بسم الله الرحمن الرحيم

In the name of Allāh,

Most Gracious, Most Merciful.

Al-Arbaʿin al-Nawawiyya:

The Forty Hadiths of Imam Nawawi

Al-Arbaʿin al-Nawawiyya: The Forty Hadiths of Imam Nawawi

MUḤYĪ AL-DĪN
YAḤYĀ IBN SHARAF AL-NAWAWĪ

With an abridgment of al-Nawawī's own commentary

Translated by
KHALID WILLIAMS

IHYA
PUBLISHING

Printed and Bound in Republic of Turkey

First edition Ihya Publishing, 2022.

ISBN 978-1-939256-09-6 (Paperback)
Library of Congress Control Number

Published by
IHYA PUBLISHING
P.O. Box 426
Alburtis, PA-18011
www.ihyapublishing.com
info@ihyapublishing.com

Title	Forty Hadith Compiled by Imam Al-Nawawi
Author	Yahya Ibn Sharaf Al-Nawawi
Commentary	Yahya Ibn Sharaf Al-Nawawi
Translation	Khalid Williams
Editing	Muhammad Isa Waley
General Editor	Athar Jatoi
Typography	ARM (www.whitethreadpress.com)

Distributed by
Muslim Publishers Group
www.mpgbooks.com
info@mpgbooks.com
+1 (844) 674-2665

Ihya Publishing is a non-profit 501(c)(3) publishing house.

Contents

اللهم صلّ على سيّدنا محمّد وسلّم

TRANSLITERATION KEY

ء (أإ)	’ (A slight catch in the breath. It is also used to indicate where the *hamza* has been dropped from the beginning of a word.)
ا	a, ā
ب	b
ت	t
ث	th (Should be pronounced as the *th* in *thin* or *thirst*.)
ج	j
ح	ḥ (Tensely breathed *h* sound.)
خ	kh (Pronounced like the *ch* in Scottish *loch* with the mouth hollowed to produce a full sound.)
د	d
ذ	dh (Should be pronounced as the *th* in *this* or *that*.)
ر	r
ز	z
س	s
ش	sh
ص	ṣ (A heavy *s* pronounced far back in the mouth with the mouth hollowed to produce a full sound.)
ض	ḍ (A heavy *d/dh* pronounced far back in the mouth with the mouth hollowed to produce a full sound.)
ط	ṭ (A heavy *t* pronounced far back in the mouth with the mouth hollowed to produce a full sound.)
ظ	ẓ (A heavy *dh* pronounced far back in the mouth with the mouth hollowed to produce a full sound.)
ع	ʿ, ʿa, ʿi, ʿu (Pronounced from the throat.)
غ	gh (Pronounced like a throaty French *r* with the mouth hollowed to produce a full sound.)
ف	f
ق	q (A guttural *q* sound with the mouth hollowed to produce a full sound.)
ك	k
ل	l
م	m
ن	n
و	w, ū, u.
ه	h
ي	y, ī, i

ﷺ	*Ṣalla ’Llāhu ʿalayhi wa sallam*—used following the mention of the Messenger Muḥammad, translated as, “May Allāh bless him and give him peace.”
عليه السلام	*ʿAlayhi ’l-salām*—used following the mention of a prophet or messenger of Allāh, translated as, “May the peace of Allāh be upon him.”
رضي الله عنه	*Raḍiya ’Llāhu ʿanhu*—used following the mention of a Companion of the Messenger ﷺ, translated as, “May Allāh be pleased with him.”
رضي الله عنها	*Raḍiya ’Llāhu ʿanhā*—used following the mention of a female Companion of the Messenger ﷺ, translated as, “May Allāh be pleased with her.”
رحمه الله	*Raḥimahu ’Llāh*—used following the mention of a scholar or pious individual, translated as, “May Allāh have mercy on him.”
رحمهم الله	*Raḥimahumu ’Llāh*—used following the mention of more than one scholar or pious individual, translated as, “May Allāh have mercy on them.”

Below format has been used for referencing Ḥadīth from one of the six authentic Ḥadīth collections to keep brevity in the text.

Bukhārī (H.B), Muslim (H.M), Abū Dāwūd (H.D), Tirimidhī (H.T), Nasā’ī (H.N), Ibn Mājah (H.I)

Author's Introduction

In the Name of God, Most Merciful and Compassionate.

Praise be to God, the Lord of the Worlds, the Sustainer of the heavens and earths, the Director of everything in creation. He sent the Messengers, may His peace and blessings be upon them all, to guide humanity and make the laws of His religion known to them through conclusive proofs and clear arguments. I praise Him for all His favors, and ask Him to extend His grace and generosity. I bear witness that there is no god but God, alone without partner; the One, the Subjugator, the Generous, the Forgiving. I bear witness that our master Muḥammad is His servant and Messenger, His beloved intimate friend, the best of His creation. He honored him with the glorious Qur'an, the enduring miracle across the ages, and with the Sunna that provides illumination to those seeking guidance; our master Muḥammad, singled out for the distinction of all-encompassing concision of discourse and the all-embracing religion. May the blessings and peace of God be upon him, and upon all the Prophets and Messengers and their families, and upon all the righteous.

Now to proceed. It has been transmitted to us from ʿAlī ibn Abī Ṭālib, ʿAbd Allāh ibn Masʿūd, Muʿādh ibn Jabal, Abū al-Dardāʾ, Ibn ʿUmar, Ibn ʿAbbās, Anas ibn Mālik, Abū Hurayra, and Abū Saʿīd al-Khudrī—may God be pleased with them all—through several chains of transmission and various narrations, that the Messenger of God ﷺ said, "Whoever preserves forty hadiths for my Community concerning their religion, God will raise him on the Day of Resurrection in the company of the folk of profound understanding and knowledge." Another narration has, "God will raise him as a person of profound understanding and knowledge." The narration of Abū al-Dardāʾ adds, "and on the Day of Resurrection I shall be his intercessor and witness." Ibn Masʿūd's narration adds, "he will be told, 'Enter through whichever gate of Paradise you please.'" Ibn ʿUmar's adds, "he will be recorded as being among the company of the folk of knowledge, and raised in the company of the martyrs."

The hadith masters agree that this is a weak narration despite its many chains of transmission; nonetheless, it has inspired many to produce Forty Hadiths collections. To my knowledge the first of them was ʿAbd Allāh ibn al-Mubārak, then Ibn Aslam al-Ṭūsī, then Ḥasan ibn Sufyān al-Nasāʾī, Abū Bakr al-Ājurrī, Abū Bakr Muḥammad ibn Ibrāhīm al-Aṣfahānī, al-Dāraquṭnī, al-Ḥākim, Abū Nuʿaym, Abū ʿAbd al-Raḥmān al-Sulamī, Abū Saʿīd al-Mālīnī, Abū ʿUthmān al-Ṣābūnī, ʿAbd Allāh ibn Muḥammad al-Anṣārī, Abū Bakr al-Bayhaqī, and countless others over the years.

By way of following in the footsteps of these great imams, I asked God to guide me in compiling a Forty Hadith collection of my own. There is scholarly consensus that it is permitted to act on weak hadiths in matters of virtuous conduct; but in any case, I rely not on the hadith in question but on the authentically transmitted sayings of the Prophet ﷺ, "Let those who are present convey to those who are absent;" and "May God make radiant anyone who hears my words, remembers them, and conveys them, just as he heard them."

Some of those who compiled Forty Hadith collections did so [according to subject categories]: on religious fundamentals, on secondary matters, on jihad, on asceticism, on rules of behavior, on preaching, and so on. All of these were for righteous purposes, and my God be pleased with those who undertook them. However, I decided to attempt something of greater importance than all of those: to compile forty hadiths containing that range of subjects in its entirety, each hadith representing a major foundation of the religion which the learned have described as having pivotal importance in Islam, ones that some had described as representing half, a third, or suchlike, of all Islam. Moreover, there was a rule that those forty hadiths be rigorously authentic (*ṣaḥīḥ*), most being drawn from the *Ṣaḥīḥ* collections of al-Bukhārī and Muslim. I chose to omit their chains of transmission to make them easy to memorize and of more general benefit, God Most High willing. Each is followed by a short commentary explaining any unusual words in them.

All who seek good in the Hereafter would do well to acquaint themselves with these hadiths, for they contain many important teachings and draw attention to all manner of forms of obedience to God, as will be obvious to anyone who contemplates them.

I place my reliance in God and depend on Him alone. All praise is His, and all favor, success, and protection come from Him.

About the Author

Imām Yaḥyā Abū Zakariyya Muḥyī al-Dīn b. Sharaf al-Nawawī, may God grant him mercy, was one of the most celebrated scholars in Islamic history. Imām al-Dhahabī, a great master of *ḥadīth*, referred to Imām al-Nawawī with the following honorary titles: the great legal authority of the Prophetic community (*Muftī al-Umma*), the authority in Prophetic tradition (*Shaykh al-Islām al-Ḥāfiẓ*), the head jurist of the Shāfiʿī school (*al-Faqīh al-Shāfiʿī*); and he described him as an ascetic (*zāhid*), and one of the towering authorities (*aḥad al-aʿlām*).[1] He reported that his shaykh, Ibn Faraḥ, said: "Shaykh Muḥyī al-Dīn [al-Nawawī] reached three high stations, each of which would suffice to make its possessor someone people would travel to see: knowledge, abstinence, and enjoining good and forbidding evil."[2]

LIFE

Childhood

Imām al-Nawawī was born in the village of Nawa in Syria in the year 631/1233. From an early age, God honored him with many saintly miracles (*karāmāt*). A virtuous saintly figure said, "it was written that he be born among the righteous."[3] Al-Nawawī's father, Sharaf al-Dīn al-Nawawī, was a righteous Sufi who observed signs of exceptional intelligence in his son from early childhood and was determined to provide him with an education that would allow him to reach his full potential. By the age of ten, Imām al-Nawawī had memorized the Holy Qurʾān.[4]

Education

At the age of eighteen, in the year 649/1251, Imām al-Nawawī moved to Damascus to continue his education.[5] He started his studies at the Sārimiyya school under the auspices of Tāj al-Dīn al-Firkāḥ (d. 690/1291), a teacher of many of the jurists and judges of Damascus. Imām al-Nawawī later moved to the Rawaḥiyya school and joined the renowned scholar, Isḥāq b. Aḥmad b. al-Maghribī (d. 650/1252), who accommodated him in a small house which became his permanent residence for the rest of his life.[6] Al-Maghribī was an expert jurist and authority in the Shāfiʿī school of law (*madhhab*) who lectured in association with Ibn al-Ṣalāḥ for twenty years. Al-Maghribī had a tremendous effect on his student; al-Nawawī was influenced by al-Maghribī's humble lifestyle and his refusal to accept many attractive offers for prestigious positions.

Al-Nawawī was a dedicated student. He attended over a dozen classes a day, including jurisprudence (*fiqh*), in which he studied the text *al-Wasīṭ* by Imām al-Ghazālī and *al-Muhadhdhab fī fiqh al-Shāfiʿī* by AbūIsḥāq Ibrāhīm al-Shirāzī, and Prophetic tradition (*ḥadīth*), in which he studied *al-Jāmiʿ bayn al-Ṣaḥīḥayn* and *Ṣaḥīḥ Muslim*. He also took daily classes in the methodology of jurisprudence (*uṣūl al-fiqh*), studying *al-Lumaʿ*, written by AbūIsḥāq al-Shīrāzī and *al-Muntakhab* by Fakhr al-Dīn al-Rāzī. In addition, he attended classes in the biographical sciences of the *ḥadīth* narrators (*ʿilm al-rijāl*) and the fundamental principles of the faith (*uṣūl al-dīn*). This extensive schedule of study required a minimum of twelve hours each day to complete.[7]

His Teachers

Al-Nawawī studied with the prominent scholars of his era, including ʿAbd al-ʿAzīz b. Muḥammad al-Anṣārī, Qāḍī ʿAbd al-Karīm b. Muḥammad al-Harastānī, and Zayn al-Dīn b. ʿAbd al-Dāʾim. Al-Nawawī learned *fiqh* under many distinguished jurists (*fuqahāʾ*), some of whom were educated by Ibn al-Ṣalāḥ or his associates. The following were among his teachers:

ʿAbd al-Raḥmān al-Maqdisī (d. 654/1256) was a towering authority and jurist who had a profound understanding of *al-Muhadhdhab* and held a long-term teaching position at the Rawāḥiyya school. In addition to his vast knowledge, he possessed fine virtues such as piety, austerity, and devotion to the worship of God ﷻ. He was the Grand Muftī of Damascus.

Imām al-Nawawī studied the methodology of *ḥadīth* (*uṣūl al-ḥadīth*) under the authority of Abū Isḥāq Ibrāhīm b. ʿIsā al-Murādī. Under his supervision, al-Nawawī completed his commentary on the *Ṣaḥīḥ* of Muslim and read the *Ṣaḥīḥ* of Bukhārī. Al-Nawawī greatly admired al-Murādī and described him as a master in *ḥadīth* and its sciences. He also had an extensive background in Sufism. Imām al-Nawawī said that he never saw anything in him that would invite criticism; he knew him as a courteous person with a tolerant nature whose affection and care for Muslims was beyond description.[8]

Sīllār b. al-Ḥasan al-Irbilī (d. 670/1272) was the Grand Muftī of Greater Syria[9] during al-Nawawī's time and a leading authority in the Shāfiʿī *madhhab.*

Qāḍī Abū al-Fatḥ al-Tiflīsī (d. 672/1274) educated Imām al-Nawawī in *uṣūl al-fiqh*, specifically in *al-Muntakhab* and part of the *Muṣṭaṣfā* of Imām al-Ghazālī. He held the office of Chief Justice (*Qāḍī al-Quḍāt*).

ʿImād al-Dīn ʿAbd al-Karīm b. Harastānī (d. 662/1264) was a scholar, teacher, judge, and a *muftī*. He replaced Ibn al-Ṣalāḥ at Dāral-Ḥadīth al-Ashrafiyya.

ʿUmar b. Asad al-Irbilī (d. 675/1276) was one of Ibn al-Ṣalāḥ's associate lecturers at Rawāḥiyya school, where he instructed Imām al-Nawawī. He was a devout Muslim and an expert in the Shāfiʿī *madhhab.* In addition to teaching, he held a position as judge. Imām al-Nawawī held him in high esteem; he used to carry his water jug and assist him in daily chores.

ʿAbd al-ʿAzīz al-Anṣārī (d. 662/1264) was an authority in literature, poetry, and many fields of Islamic sciences. Al-Anṣārī was a distinguished and influential scholar. While he had strong ties with kings and nobility, he never neglected the needs of the people.[10]

SCHOLARSHIP

Imām al-Nawawī completed his education at the age of twenty-five and began to write books in a variety of disciplines. He wrote on *fiqh, ḥadīth,* and *ʿaqīda* (creed). In addition, he became a public figure guiding Muslims—rulers and citizens alike. Imām al-Nawawī continued to strengthen his self-discipline by focusing on the heart, observing its states, functions, and conditions, holding himself accountable for every thought that crossed his mind, and consciously thinking of ways to purify his heart.

Fiqh

Imām al-Nawawī studied the Shāfiʿī *madhhab* under the most prestigious scholars of his time. In a very short period, he mastered the foundations, methodologies, and principles of the *madhhab*. Subsequently, he became the highest authority of his time and was called the authoritative redactor (*muḥarrir*) of the Shāfiʿī *madhhab*. Imām al-Nawawī's books became important sources for *muftīs* and judges. *Fatwās* were based on his books, and scholars expanded and abridged them. Scholars agreed that Imām al-Nawawī had reached a rank such that he was capable of inferring expert legal rulings from foundational proofs; that is, he could exercise *ijtīhād* when issuing *fatwās*. Imām al-Suyūṭī (d. 911/1505), the polymath, jurist, and renewer (*mujaddid*), said, "When I reached the level of complete discernment, I did not issue a *fatwā* without having consulted al-Nawawī's books, even when I had already viewed others I regarded as preponderant."[11] Al-Asnawī wrote, "Al-Nawawī is the *muḥarrir* of the *madhhab*: he examined it, revised it, and organized it;"[12] Ibn Kathīr stated that "al-Nawawī is the shaykh of the [Shāfiʿī] *madhhab* and the head of the jurists of his time."[13]

Hadith

Imām al-Nawawī was a scholar of ḥadīth (*muḥaddith*) and a master in its sciences; he was one of the pillars in this field, at the rank of towering authorities such as Ibn al-Ṣalāḥ, al-Mizzī, al-Dhahabī, and Ibn Ḥajar, whose scholarship contributed tremendously to the development of the science of *ḥadīth*. It is an understatement to say that Imām al-Nawawī was an exceptional scholar;[14] in fact, it is rare to find a scholar who combined the two main fields in the Islamic sciences of *fiqh* and *ḥadīth*. Imām al-Nawawī narrated the following books from their sources, through their chain of authority (*sanad*), to those who authored them: *Ṣaḥīḥ al-Bukhārī; Ṣaḥīḥ Muslim*; the *Sunans* of Abū Dāwūd, al-Tirmidhī, and al-Nasāʾī, the *Muwaṭṭaʾ* of Mālik; the *Musnad* of al-Shāfiʿī; the *Mūsnads* of Ibn Ḥanbal, al-Dārimī, al-Isfarāyinī, and Abū Yaʿlā; and the *Sunans* of Ibn Māja, al-Dāraquṭnī, al-Bayhaqī, al-Baghāwī and others. Imām al-Nawawī insisted that the five main books that contain the foundations of Islam are the two *Ṣaḥīḥs* of Bukhārī and Muslim, and the *Sunans* of Abū Dāwūd, al-Tirmidhī, and al-Nasāʾī.[15] He was knowledgeable in all of the categories related to assessing the authenticity of *ḥadīth*[16] and established many of the later conventions required for its study.[17]

Imām al-Nawawī was also an authority on the science of the narrators of *ḥadīth* (*ʿilm al-rijāl*). He studied *al-Kamāl fī asmāʾ al-rijāl* with Shaykh Abū al-Baqā al-Nābulusī.[18] In addition, he attained a firm knowledge of the transmitters of *ḥadīth*, particularly what is known as "the high chain" (*al-sanad al-ʿālī*). In order for a *ḥadīth* to be included in this chain, there must be the fewest possible number of transmitters leading back to the Prophet Muḥammad ﷺ; the fewer the number of transmitters, the more authentic the *ḥadīth*. In addition to establishing the major topics pertaining to the discipline of *fiqh al-ḥadīth*, in an effort to help readers understand this field of Islamic sciences,[19] Imām al-Nawawī also established the rules that should be followed by those who narrate *ḥadīth*.[20]

Arabic Linguistics

Imām al-Nawawī was a master of the Arabic language. He became completely proficient in its grammar, morphology, and syntax (*al-ṣarf wa al-naḥw*), its lexical derivations, and diction.[21] He also clarified homonyms, defined them, and explained their differences.[22]

Creed

None of al-Nawawī's teachers specialized in creed (*ʿaqīda*), but all those mentioned were Sunnī Muslims of Ahl al-Sunna wa al-Jamāʿa. It is clear from Imām al-Nawawī's books, however, that he was an Ashʿarī. The Ashʿariyya took their name from the founder, Abū al-Ḥasan ʿAlī b. Ismāʿīl al-Ashʿarī (260–324/874–936). Al-Ashʿarī was a Sunnī theologian who believed that God ﷻ, among other things, has distinctive ontological attributes such as life, knowledge, will, power, sight, hearing, and speech. Imām al-Nawawī wrote a short book on the unity of God (*tawḥīd*) titled *al-Maqāṣid*. This book reflects Imām al-Nawawī's understanding of the *ʿaqīda* of Sunnī Islam.[23]

Works

Imām al-Nawawī began writing at an early stage of his life and left a huge legacy. His ambition to write was so great that he was known to write many books simultaneously. The vast number of books that he wrote (it has been reported that he wrote more than fifty works ranging from short treatises to encyclopedic volumes) is evidence of God's blessings. His books were tremendously popular, both during and after his lifetime; they have been published, translated, and distributed around the world. Even today, a great many Muslim households have at least one book written by Imām al-Nawawī.[24]

Sufism

Imām al-Nawawī's life, conduct, and writings indicate that he followed the ways of the righteous Sufis who embodied purity and honesty in their sayings and deeds. His book *Bustān al-ʿārifīn* is a small text that illustrates his focus on sincerity and the need to transcend worldly life.

Imām al-Nawawī's complete awe of God ﷻ was his first level of Sufism (*taṣawwuf*). When some students asked him to write a book on asceticism (*zuhd*), his reply was: "I wrote for you a book concerning the rules of trade (*buyūʿ*)." This reply indicates that genuine *zuhd* is to avoid all that God ﷻ made unlawful and refrain from unjustly oppressing others. Imām al-Nawawī practiced this by abstaining from eating doubtful food provided by the school where he studied. Later, when he became a teacher, he declined a salary for his service. He also refused to eat any food from Damascus because many of its endowed properties (*awqāf*) had been misappropriated.[25] Imām al-Nawawī was content with a minimal amount of food and survived on the bread and olives that his father used to send him from Nawā. He would not waste time cooking and eating; rather, he continually occupied himself in learning, teaching, and worshiping. Ibn Kathīr reported that al-Nawawī fasted his whole life.[26] He ate one meal a day after the *ʿishā* prayer and had one drink of water at dawn. Fruit and chilled water to him were wasteful extravagances. Ibn al-Muʿallim said that he saw a man peel a cucumber and offer it to Imām al-Nawawī, who politely declined and apologized, explaining: "I fear that it would satiate my body and might cause me to sleep."[27] Ibn al-ʿAṭṭār quoted Shaykh Muḥammad al-Anṣārī as saying that "If al-Qushayrī [the author of al-Risāla, who lived generations before Imām al-Nawawī] had had the chance to know Imām al-Nawawī and his shaykh, al-Maghribī, he would have placed them at the top of his list of the righteous and sanctified Sufis."[28] As we have seen, Imām al-Nawawī was a master scholar in Sharīʿa, the outward sciences, but he combined this with *taṣawwuf*, the science of moral perfection (*iḥsān*). He writes in his short book entitled *al-Maqāṣid fī' al-tawḥīd wa al-ʿibāda wa uṣūl al-taṣawwuf* that the Way of the Sufis has five principles:

1. keep the presence of God ﷻ in your heart in public and in private;
2. follow the Sunna of the Prophet ﷺ in actions and speech;
3. avoid the unnecessary company of people and asking anything of them;
4. be happy with what God ﷻ has given you, even if it is little; and
5. always turn your personal business over to God ﷻ.[29]

The Imām incorporated his knowledge of Islam in the practice of Sufism out of the fear and love of God ﷻ. There is no practice without knowledge, and no knowledge without practice. Because Imām al-Nawawī sincerely practiced all that he knew, God filled his words with profound wisdom and lasting blessings. Because he led such an ascetic life of self-denial, many of his contemporaries and peers were concerned about his health. When they expressed their worries to him, Imām al-Nawawī appreciated their good intentions, but did not act upon their concerns. He had no interest in this worldly life; to him this life was a short transitory path to eternal existence with God ﷻ.

Imām al-Nawawī did not accept gifts from anyone except those who were known for their piety and sincere knowledge. He believed that it was his duty to propagate knowledge without any material reward. On one rare occasion, he accepted a pair of sandals offered to him by a Sufi and received a water jug from another Sufi, neither of whom were among his students. This happened toward the end of his life. His acceptance of these gifts was significant: his life was almost over and the sandals and the jug are travelers' items—signs indicating his final journey. Although Imām al-Nawawī deprived himself of delicious foods, he permitted other people to eat them. He declared that eating delicacies and delicious foods was not a violation of asceticism. He wrote in his commentary on *Ṣaḥīḥ* Muslim that the Prophet ﷺ used to like sweet foods and honey.[30]

Imām al-Nawawī dressed in simple clothing. He wore a small cap and an ankle-length outer garment. His beard was black with a few gray hairs; he was of medium height with brown skin. His demeanor invited calmness and his appearance imposed respect. During discussions and conversations, he never used a loud tone of voice like other scholars; instead he spoke in a quiet and soft manner. He used to open his speeches by praising God ﷻ and thanking Him. If the Prophet Muḥammad ﷺ was mentioned, he would invoke aloud the blessings and prayers of God ﷻ upon him. He mentioned righteous people with dignity and respect and used honorary titles before their names. Imām al-Nawawī never married, and, as indicated earlier, never owned a large or comfortable house; he continued living all his life in the first room he had been given in the Rawāḥiyya school.

Holding the Ruler Accountable

Although Imām al-Nawawī occupied himself in teaching, writing, and worship, he did not isolate himself from society; rather he put himself at the service of the people. He continually made Islam's demands for social justice known to the powerful. The sultan of his time was Baybars, the formidable Mamluk ruler of Egypt and Greater Syria who crushed the Mongols in the famous battle of *ʿAyn Jālūt* in Palestine, on Friday 25 Ramaḍān 658/3 September 1260. Baybars also inflicted a devastating defeat on King Louis ix of France, thus ultimately removing the foreign threat of both the Mongols and Crusaders. Toward the end of his reign, Sultan Baybars and Imām al-Nawawī had a famous public disagreement. Sultan Baybars had placed a heavy tax on the people to finance his continued campaigns against the Mongols and the crusaders. He asked the scholars to issue a legal judgment (*fatwā*) that justified his taxation policy, and all but Imām al-Nawawī acquiesced. Baybars invited al-Nawawī to his palace and asked him to sign the *fatwā*. Imām al-Nawawī refused to sign the document and said:

> I have heard that you have one thousand slaves and each one of them possesses a large amount of gold. In addition, you own two hundred concubines, and each of them has a vessel full of jewelry.

> If you donate all these treasures to fund your campaigns, I will give you a legal judgment (*fatwā*) to collect your taxes from the people.[31]

In his anger, Sultan Baybars ordered the Imām to leave Damascus. Al-Nawawī replied, "I hear and obey" and returned to Nawā. The scholars urged the sultan to reconsider. Later, the sultan wrote to Imām al-Nawawī, requesting him to come back to Damascus. Imām al-Nawawī replied, "I will never enter Damascus as long as Baybars is in it." Less than a month later, Sultan Baybars died and al-Nawawī returned to Damascus.[32]

Imām al-Nawawī's Death

After twenty-eight extraordinarily productive years in Damascus, Imām al-Nawawī returned to his hometown of Nawā. He returned the books he had borrowed from the school library, visited his teachers' graves, made supplication for their souls, and cried. He then visited his living friends and bid them farewell.

On Wednesday the twenty-fourth of Rajab (676/1277) at the age of forty-five, Imām al-Nawawī died. He was mourned far and wide. Among the many contemporary eulogies that were written for him are the following lines:

We grieve over your loss, a bane for us all.
Death finished our hopes of a long life for you.
The dawn and the sunset are lonely times,
ruined by the lack of your friendly presence.
You recited God's Book with tears in your eyes,
repeating it over and over again;
monotony never came close to you.
For the Faith you were a guiding light.
Your words and deeds will endure forever.[33]

Imām al-Nawawī lives on today in the hearts of Muslims everywhere. His works are of everlasting value. May God ﷻ shower him with His mercy and reward him for his great service to Islam and its sciences.

HADITH 1

Actions are Defined by Intentions

عَنْ أَمِيرِ الْمُؤْمِنِيْنَ أَبِي حَفْصٍ عُمَرَ بْنِ الْخَطَّابِ رَضِيَ اللّٰهُ عَنْهُ قَالَ: سَمِعْتُ رَسُولَ اللّٰهِ صَلَّى اللّٰهُ عَلَيْهِ وَسَلَّمَ يَقُولُ:

«إِنَّمَا الْأَعْمَالُ بِالنِّيَّاتِ، وَإِنَّمَا لِكُلِّ امْرِئٍ مَا نَوَى، فَمَنْ كَانَتْ هِجْرَتُهُ إِلَى اللّٰهِ وَرَسُولِهِ فَهِجْرَتُهُ إِلَى اللّٰهِ وَرَسُوْلِهِ، وَمَنْ كَانَتْ هِجْرَتُهُ لِدُنْيَا يُصِيبُهَا أَوْ امْرَأَةٍ يَنْكِحُهَا فَهِجْرَتُهُ إِلَى مَا هَاجَرَ إِلَيْهِ».

It is related from the Commander of the Believers Abū Ḥafṣ ʿUmar ibn al-Khaṭṭāb ﷺ that he heard the Prophet ﷺ say:

"Actions are defined by intentions alone, and each person will have just what they intend. If someone emigrates to God and His Messenger, his emigration is to God and His Messenger. If someone emigrates for some worldly gain, or to marry a woman, his emigration is for that to which he emigrates." [Bukhārī 1, Muslim 1907]

Commentary

The hadith shows that intention is the yardstick of the deed: if the intention is sound, the deed is sound in God's sight. The nature of a sound intention is threefold: some worship God out of fear of Him, like slaves. Others worship Him out of desire for Paradise and reward, like traders. Then there are those who worship Him simply because it is right to give Him thanks and worship, though they are aware of their shortcomings in fulfilling this right, which is the worship of the noble. This is what the Prophet ﷺ demonstrated when ʿĀʾisha ﷺ asked why he stood in prayer at night until his feet swelled up, though God had already granted him forgiveness for the past and the future, and he replied, "Should I not, then, be a grateful servant?"

In answer to the question of whether it is better to worship with fear or with hope, al-Ghazālī said that hope is better, for hope produces love while fear may lead to despair.

Sound intention in worship may be vitiated by self-satisfaction and pride, desire for worldly gain, or showing off. All of these amount to setting up a partner to God in one's worship. The Prophet ﷺ told us that God says, "I have no need whatsoever of partners. If someone does a need for Me and for someone else too, I disown it." Al-Muḥāsibī says in *al-Riʿāya* that sincerity means to obey God out of desire for Him alone and nothing else. Al-Marzubānī said that if a prayer is to be raised up to God it must be performed with four things: a present heart, an attentive mind, the requisite actions, and a humble body.

Imām al-Nawawī identifies six different meanings for *hijra* (emigration), and states that the basic concept is that of separating oneself from something for a purpose.

HADITH 2

Islām, Īmān, and Iḥsān

عَنْ عُمَرَ رَضِيَ اللّٰهُ عَنْهُ أَيْضًا قَالَ:

«بَيْنَمَا نَحْنُ جُلُوْسٌ عِنْدَ رَسُوْلِ اللّٰهِ صَلَّى اللّٰهُ عَلَيْهِ وَسَلَّمَ ذَاتَ يَوْمٍ، إِذْ طَلَعَ عَلَيْنَا رَجُلٌ شَدِيْدُ بَيَاضِ الثِّيَابِ، شَدِيْدُ سَوَادِ الشَّعْرِ، لَا يُرَى عَلَيْهِ أَثَرُ السَّفَرِ، وَلَا يَعْرِفُهُ مِنَّا أَحَدٌ. حَتَّى جَلَسَ إِلَى النَّبِيِّ صَلَّى اللّٰهُ عَلَيْهِ وَسَلَّمَ. فَأَسْنَدَ رُكْبَتَيْهِ إِلَى رُكْبَتَيْهِ، وَوَضَعَ كَفَّيْهِ عَلَى فَخِذَيْهِ، وَقَالَ: يَا مُحَمَّدُ أَخْبِرْنِيْ عَنِ الْإِسْلَامِ. فَقَالَ رَسُولُ اللّٰهِ صَلَّى اللّٰهُ عَلَيْهِ وَسَلَّمَ: الْإِسْلَامُ أَنْ تَشْهَدَ أَنْ لَا إِلَهَ إِلَّا اللّٰهُ وَأَنَّ مُحَمَّدًا رَسُوْلُ اللّٰهِ، وَتُقِيْمَ الصَّلَاةَ، وَتُؤْتِيَ الزَّكَاةَ، وَتَصُوْمَ رَمَضَانَ، وَتَحُجَّ الْبَيْتَ إِنْ اسْتَطَعْتَ إِلَيْهِ سَبِيْلًا. قَالَ: صَدَقْتَ . فَعَجِبْنَا لَهُ يَسْأَلُهُ وَيُصَدِّقُهُ! قَالَ: فَأَخْبِرْنِيْ عَنِ الْإِيْمَانِ. قَالَ: أَنْ تُؤْمِنَ بِاللّٰهِ وَمَلَائِكَتِهِ وَكُتُبِهِ وَرُسُلِهِ وَالْيَوْمِ الْآخِرِ، وَتُؤْمِنَ بِالْقَدْرِ خَيْرِهِ وَشَرِّهِ. قَالَ: صَدَقْتَ. قَالَ: فَأَخْبِرْنِيْ عَنِ الْإِحْسَانِ. قَالَ: أَنْ تَعْبُدَ اللّٰهَ

كَأَنَّكَ تَرَاهُ، فَإِنْ لَمْ تَكُنْ تَرَاهُ فَإِنَّهُ يَرَاكَ. قَالَ: فَأَخْبِرْنِيْ عَنِ السَّاعَةِ. قَالَ: مَا الْمَسْئُوْلُ عَنْهَا بِأَعْلَمَ مِنَ السَّائِلِ. قَالَ: فَأَخْبِرْنِيْ عَنْ أَمَارَاتِهَا؟ قَالَ: أَنْ تَلِدَ الْأَمَةُ رَبَّتَهَا، وَأَنْ تَرَى الْحُفَاةَ الْعُرَاةَ الْعَالَةَ رِعَاءَ الشَّاءِ يَتَطَاوَلُوْنَ فِي الْبُنْيَانِ. ثُمَّ انْطَلَقَ، فَلَبِثْتُ مَلِيًّا، ثُمَّ قَالَ: يَا عُمَرُ أَتَدْرِيْ مَنِ السَّائِلُ؟. قُلْتُ: اللّٰهُ وَرَسُوْلُهُ أَعْلَمُ. قَالَ: فَإِنَّهُ جِبْرِيْلُ أَتَاكُمْ يُعَلِّمُكُمْ دِيْنَكُمْ».

ʿUmar ﵁ also related:

"One day we were sitting with the Messenger of God ﷺ when a man came along wearing very white clothes, and with very black hair. He did not appear to have been travelling, yet none of us knew him. He sat down knee-to-knee with the Prophet ﷺ, placed his hands on his thighs, and said, 'Muḥammad, tell me what is submission (*islām*).' The Messenger of God ﷺ replied, 'Submission is to testify that there is no god but God and that Muḥammad is the Messenger of God, and to observe prayer, to give zakat, to fast Ramaḍān, and to perform pilgrimage to the House [of God] if able to make the journey.'

"'You have spoken truly," he said. We were astonished at how he questioned him and then approved his answer.

"He then asked, 'Now tell me what is faith (*īmān*).' The Prophet ﷺ replied, 'It is to believe in God, His Angels, His Books, His Messengers, and the Last Day, and to believe in destiny both good and bad.' The man said, 'You have spoken truly.'

"He then asked, 'Now tell me what is excellence (*iḥsān*).' He replied, 'It is to worship God as if you see Him; for if you see Him not, He sees you.'

"He then asked, 'Now tell me of the [Last] Hour.' He replied, 'The one asked knows no more about it than the one asking.' The man said, 'Then tell me of its portents.' He replied, 'That a slave-girl gives birth to her mistress, and you see barefoot, naked, destitute shepherds competing in the construction of tall buildings.'

"The stranger then departed. We remained silent for a while, and then [the Prophet] asked, "Umar, do you know who that was?' I replied, 'God and His Messenger know best.' He said, 'It was Gabriel. He came to teach you your religion.'" [Muslim 8]

Commentary

The hadith distinguishes between faith (*īmān*), which means belief, and submission (*islām*), which means action. God makes this same distinction in the Qur'an: *The Bedouin say, 'We believe.' Say: 'You do not believe; but say, "We submit", for faith has not yet entered your hearts* [Q. 49:14]. For it is one thing to speak words and perform actions with one's outward body, and another thing to believe things with one's inner heart.

Regarding "destiny (*qadar*), both good and bad", the true teaching of our religion is that destiny is a reality, and that God decreed all things before time began, and knows when and where all things will occur in the manner in which He decreed them. Yet although destiny as He knows it is inevitable, the decree written upon the Preserved Tablet can change, for God says, *God effaces and confirms what He will, and in His keeping is the Mother of the Book* [Q. 13:39]. Ibn ʿUmar ﵄ used to pray, "Dear God, if You have written that I be among the damned, then erase me and write that I be among the saved." A hadith says, "Charity and keeping family ties ward off a bad death and change it into a good one." Another hadith says, "Supplications and tribulations are engaged in mortal combat between heaven and earth, and a supplication may drive off a tribulation before it can descend."

"Excellence (*iḥsān*) is to worship God as if you see Him; for if you see Him not, He sees you." This is the station of witnessing; for if you could see God, you would be ashamed to look away from Him while praying, or to let your heart become engrossed in anything but Him.

The Prophet's ﷺ answer "The one asked knows no more of it than the one asking" indicates that knowledge of the Hour is something that God has kept to Himself. We do not know how much time our world has left, despite what some may claim.

The Prophet's ﷺ words "He came to teach you your religion" prove that faith, submission, and spiritual excellence together make up our religion.

The hadith affirms that belief in destiny it is obligatory, and that we must be content with our destinies. A man asked Imam Aḥmad ibn Ḥanbal for advice, and he replied, "God has taken care of your provision, so why worry? God has sworn to repay you in full, so why be stingy? Paradise is real, so why take it easy? The interrogation of Munkar and Nakīr in the grave is real, so why feel comfortable? The world will come to an end, so why feel secure in it? The Reckoning is real, so why be acquisitive? Everything comes down to destiny and fate, so why be fearful?"

In this world some things come about through intermediary causes, some without them. In any case, all are determined by divine decree.

HADITH 3

The Pillars of Islam

عَنْ أَبِي عَبْدِ الرَّحْمٰنِ عَبْدِ اللّٰهِ بْنِ عُمَرَ بْنِ الْخَطَّابِ رَضِيَ اللّٰهُ عَنْهُمَا قَالَ: سَمِعْتُ رَسُوْلَ اللّٰهِ صَلَّى اللّٰهُ عَلَيْهِ وَسَلَّمَ يَقُوْلُ:

«بُنِيَ الْإِسْلَامُ عَلَى خَمْسٍ: شَهَادَةِ أَنْ لَا إِلٰهَ إِلَّا اللّٰهُ وَأَنَّ مُحَمَّدًا رَسُوْلُ اللّٰهِ، وَإِقَامِ الصَّلَاةِ، وَإِيْتَاءِ الزَّكَاةِ، وَحَجِّ الْبَيْتِ، وَصَوْمِ رَمَضَانَ».

It is related from ʿAbd Allāh ibn ʿUmar ﵄ that he reported: I heard the Prophet ﷺ say,

"Islam is built upon five things: testifying that there is no god but God and that Muḥammad is the Messenger of God, observing prayer, paying zakat, making pilgrimage to the House, and fasting Ramaḍān." [Bukhārī 8, Muslim 16]

Commentary

"Islam is built upon five things." Just as a house is completed by its pillars, Islam is made complete by these five things. The Prophet ﷺ said elsewhere, "Prayer is the main pillar of the religion, and anyone who neglects it brings down the religion." The same is true of the other pillars. God employs a similar metaphor in the Qur'an: *Is he who founds his building upon reverence for God and His good pleasure better, or he who founds his building upon the brink of a crumbling bank, so that it topples with him into the fire of Hell?* [Q. 9:109].

The five pillars listed in the hadith are the mainstays of the edifice of Islam. The rest of the building is made up of the other obligatory and recommended acts, which are like decorations. The Prophet ﷺ said in another hadith, "Faith is seventy-some branches, the highest of which is '*There is no god but God,*' and the lowest of which is clearing harmful objects from a pathway."

HADITH 4

The Stages of Human Creation

عَنْ أَبِي عَبْدِ الرَّحْمٰنِ عَبْدِ اللّٰهِ بْنِ مَسْعُوْدٍ رَضِيَ اللّٰهُ عَنْهُ قَالَ: حَدَّثَنَا رَسُوْلُ
اللّٰهِ صَلَّى اللّٰهُ عَلَيْهِ وَسَلَّمَ – وَهُوَ الصَّادِقُ الْمَصْدُوْقُ:

«إِنَّ أَحَدَكُمْ يُجْمَعُ خَلْقُهُ فِيْ بَطْنِ أُمِّهِ أَرْبَعِيْنَ يَوْمًا نُطْفَةً، ثُمَّ يَكُوْنُ
عَلَقَةً مِثْلَ ذٰلِكَ، ثُمَّ يَكُوْنُ مُضْغَةً مِثْلَ ذٰلِكَ، ثُمَّ يُرْسَلُ إِلَيْهِ الْمَلَكُ فَيَنْفُخُ
فِيهِ الرُّوْحَ، وَيُؤْمَرُ بِأَرْبَعِ كَلِمَاتٍ: بِكَتْبِ رِزْقِهِ، وَأَجَلِهِ، وَعَمَلِهِ، وَشَقِيٌّ أَمْ
سَعِيدٍ؛ فَوَاللّٰهِ الَّذِي لَا إِلٰهَ غَيْرُهُ إِنَّ أَحَدَكُمْ لَيَعْمَلُ بِعَمَلِ أَهْلِ الْجَنَّةِ حَتَّى
مَا يَكُوْنُ بَيْنَهُ وَبَيْنَهَا إِلَّا ذِرَاعٌ فَيَسْبِقُ عَلَيْهِ الْكِتَابُ فَيَعْمَلُ بِعَمَلِ أَهْلِ النَّارِ
فَيَدْخُلُهَا. وَإِنَّ أَحَدَكُمْ لَيَعْمَلُ بِعَمَلِ أَهْلِ النَّارِ حَتَّى مَا يَكُوْنُ بَيْنَهُ وَبَيْنَهَا
إِلَّا ذِرَاعٌ فَيَسْبِقُ عَلَيْهِ الْكِتَابُ فَيَعْمَلُ بِعَمَلِ أَهْلِ الْجَنَّةِ فَيَدْخُلُهَا».

It is related from ʿAbd Allāh ibn Masʿūd ﵁ that he said:

"The Prophet ﷺ told us, and he is most truthful and believable,

'Each one of you is assembled in his mother's womb as a drop of fluid for forty days, then as a clot for just as long, then as a morsel of flesh for just as long. Then the angel is sent to him to breathe the spirit into him, and is commanded to write four things: his provision, his life-span, his deeds, and whether he shall be damned or saved. By God, besides whom there is no other god, truly one of you may act as if he is bound for Paradise until he is only an arm's length from it—but then what was written catches up with him, and he does the deeds of the Hell-bound and enters Hell. And another of you may act as if he is bound for Hell until he is only an arm's length from it—but then what was written catches up with him, and he does the deeds of the Paradise-bound and enters Paradise.'" [Bukhārī 3208, Muslim 2643]

Commentary

God says, *O mankind, if you are in doubt about the Resurrection, then We created you from dust, then from a drop, then from a clot, then from a morsel of flesh, formed and unformed* [Q. 22:5]. Our father Adam was created from dust, and then his progeny from a drop. The drop grows into a clot, then into a "morsel", so called because it is the size of a bite of food. Then in the third stage, God forms that morsel and gives it its sensory faculties and internal organs. God says: *He it is Who forms you in the wombs as He will* [Q. 3:6]. Then at four months, the spirit is breathed into the infant, and its destiny is written. Therefore it is said that "salvation precedes birth."

This hadith shows that one can never be certain whether someone will go to Paradise or Hell, regardless of the deeds one sees them doing. It also teaches us not to rely on our own deeds or be satisfied with them, for we do not know how things will turn out in the end. We should all ask God to grant us a good end, and seek His refuge from a bad one.

HADITH 5

Blameworthy Innovation

عَنْ أُمِّ الْمُؤْمِنِيْنَ أُمِّ عَبْدِ اللّٰهِ عَائِشَةَ رَضِيَ اللّٰهُ عَنْهَا، قَالَتْ: قَالَ: رَسُوْلُ اللّٰهِ صَلَّى اللّٰهُ عَلَيْهِ وَسَلَّمَ:

«مَنْ أَحْدَثَ فِي أَمْرِنَا هَذَا مَا لَيْسَ مِنْهُ فَهُوَ رَدٌّ وَفِي رِوَايَةٍ لِمُسْلِمٍ: مَنْ عَمِلَ عَمَلًا لَيْسَ عَلَيْهِ أَمْرُنَا فَهُوَ رَدٌّ».

The Mother of the Believers ʿĀ'isha ﷺ reported that the Prophet ﷺ said,

"If anyone introduces something in to our teachings that does not belong to them, it will be rejected."

Or, as narrated by Muslim, "If anyone performs an action that is not supported by our teachings, it will be rejected." [Bukhārī 2697, Muslim 1718]

Commentary

This hadith means that if acts of worship, such as the major or minor ablution, fasting, or prayer are performed in a manner that diverges from the Law, they will be rejected. It also means that if ownership of something is taken by means of an invalid contract, the property must be returned to its original owner. The hadith also shows that if someone introduces an innovation into the religion that does not accord with the Law, he bears the burden of its sin, his action is rejected, and he is deserving of divine punishment.

HADITH 6

Avoiding Doubtful Things

عَنْ أَبِيْ عَبْدِ اللّٰهِ النُّعْمَانِ بْنِ بَشِيْرٍ رَضِيَ اللّٰهُ عَنْهُمَا، قَالَ: سَمِعْتُ رَسُوْلَ اللّٰهِ صَلَّى اللّٰهُ عَلَيْهِ وَسَلَّمَ يَقُوْلُ: «إِنَّ الْحَلَالَ بَيِّنٌ، وَإِنَّ الْحَرَامَ بَيِّنٌ، وَبَيْنَهُمَا أُمُوْرٌ مُشْتَبِهَاتٌ لَا يَعْلَمُهُنَّ كَثِيْرٌ مِنَ النَّاسِ، فَمَنِ اتَّقَى الشُّبُهَاتِ فَقَدِ اسْتَبْرَأَ لِدِيْنِهِ وَعِرْضِهِ، وَمَنْ وَقَعَ فِي الشُّبُهَاتِ وَقَعَ فِي الْحَرَامِ، كَالرَّاعِي يَرْعَى حَوْلَ الْحِمَى يُوشِكُ أَنْ يَرْتَعَ فِيْهِ، أَلَا وَإِنَّ لِكُلِّ مَلِكٍ حِمًى، أَلَا وَإِنَّ حِمَى اللّٰهِ مَحَارِمُهُ، أَلَا وَإِنَّ فِي الْجَسَدِ مُضْغَةً إِذَا صَلَحَتْ صَلَحَ الْجَسَدُ كُلُّهُ، وَإِذَا فَسَدَتْ فَسَدَ الْجَسَدُ كُلُّهُ، أَلَا وَهِيَ الْقَلْبُ».

Al-Nuʿmān ibn Bashīr ﷺ reported that he heard the Prophet ﷺ say,

"The lawful is clear and the unlawful is clear, but between them are doubtful things unknown to many people. He who is wary of doubtful things keeps his religion and his honor blameless. He who lapses into doubtful things lapses into the unlawful, like a shepherd who herds his flock near a private enclosure, on the verge of entering it. For every king has a private enclosure, and God's private enclosure is all that He has forbidden. There is a morsel in the body: if it is sound, the whole body is sound; if it is corrupt, the whole body is corrupt. Verily it is the heart." [Bukhārī 52, Muslim 1599]

Commentary

Between the lawful and the unlawful there are doubtful things that could belong to either category. If there is no good reason to doubt something, then it should not be doubted, and indeed to enquire into it further would be a reprehensible innovation. For example, if a stranger comes along selling his wares, there is no obligation to enquire into their legal status, nor even any recommendation to do so, and one should not ask about them.

"He who is wary of doubtful things keeps his religion and his honor blameless:" his religion because he avoids doubt, and his honor because he avoids the risk of foolish people gossiping about him and accusing him of indulging in the unlawful. The Prophet ﷺ is reported to have said, "Anyone who believes in God and the Last Day should avoid things that raise other people's suspicions." ʿAlī ؓ reportedly said, "Keep clear of things that people's hearts condemn, even if you have a valid excuse, for others may hear of your actions but not your excuses."

"He who lapses into doubtful things lapses into the unlawful"—either by lapsing into the unlawful without knowing it to be unlawful, or else as a result of gradually coming closer and closer to doing so. When the soul lapses into something blameworthy, it keeps on slipping further and further into depravity by degrees.

"There is a morsel in the body. . ."—It is said that the body is a kingdom. The soul is its capital city, the heart its center, and the limbs are its workers. The inner faculties are the lamps that illuminate the city. The intellect is the minister who does his best to see to its welfare. Appetite is the porter who procures provisions for the workers. Irascibility is the police chief, a vile character who professes to be a sincere adviser, though his advice is deadly poison and he is forever trying to wrest control from the minister. The imagination, at the front of the brain, is the treasurer. Contemplation is at the center of the brain, memory at the back. The tongue is the interpreter. The five senses are emissaries, each with its own calling: the eye is assigned to the realm of color, the hearing to the real of sound, and so on. The heart, though, is king. If the ruler is sound, his subjects will be sound. If he is corrupt, so will they be. The heart can only be sound is it is protected from inward diseases such as rancor, envy, avarice, stinginess, pride, cynicism, ostentation, love of reputation, duplicity, greed, and dissatisfaction with destiny. May God protect us from all these maladies and more, so that we may come to Him with sound hearts.

HADITH 7

Religion is Sincerity

عَنْ أَبِيْ رُقَيَّةَ تَمِيْمِ بْنِ أَوْسٍ الدَّارِيِّ رَضِيَ اللّٰهُ عَنْهُ أَنَّ النَّبِيَّ صَلَّى اللّٰهُ عَلَيْهِ وَسَلَّمَ قَالَ:

«الدِّيْنُ النَّصِيحَةُ». قُلْنَا: لِمَنْ؟ قَالَ: «لِلّٰهِ، وَلِكِتَابِهِ، وَلِرَسُوْلِهِ، وَلِأَئِمَّةِ الْمُسْلِمِيْنَ وَعَامَّتِهِمْ».

It is related from Tamīm al-Dārī ﷺ that

"The Prophet ﷺ said, 'Religion is sincerity.' We asked, 'Towards whom?' He replied, 'Towards God, His Book, His Messenger, and the Muslims, both the leaders and the masses.'" [Muslim 55]

Commentary

Sincerity towards God means believing in Him and not associating any partners with Him, attributing to Him all the qualities of perfection and majesty. It means obeying Him and loving and hating for His sake. It means acknowledging His favors and giving thanks for them. It means calling others to these qualities, and showing kindness to all people as much as one is able to. Ultimately all these qualities come down to the sincere advice that you give to yourself, for it is not God who needs your sincerity, but you.

Sincerity towards the Book of God means believing that it is the Word of God, unlike any human speech and beyond human abilities. It means revering it and reciting it correctly, with humility and exactitude. It means to defend it from false interpretations and unjust attacks. It means to believe what it says, to hold to its laws, to understand its teachings and parables, to reflect upon its admonitions, and to contemplate its wonders. It means to act upon its clear edicts, and defer to its ambiguous passages. It means to acquaint oneself with which of its proclamations are universal and which are specific, and which of its passages are abrogated by others. It means to convey its teachings to others.

Sincerity towards the Messenger of God ﷺ means believing in his message and teachings, obeying his commands, supporting him in life and in death, opposing his opponents, and allying with his allies. It means revering and honoring him, and reviving and furthering his Sunna. It means learning and teaching his Sunna to others with kindness, reverence, and respect. It means adorning oneself with his character and ethics. It means loving his Family and Companions. It means avoiding those who innovate in his Sunna or speak ill of any of his Companions.

Sincerity towards Muslim leaders means helping and obeying them in the cause of truth, and gently reminding them of it. It means informing them of the rights of their fellow Muslims if they are unaware of them. It means to refrain from rebelling against them, and to work to unite the hearts of one's fellow Muslims in obedience to them. According to al-Khaṭṭābī it also means to pray behind them, fight alongside them, deliver the zakat to them, refrain from violent insurrection against them even if they rule unjustly, not to flatter them with false praise, and to pray that they be guided.

HADITH 8

The Inviolability of the Muslim's Blood and Property

عَنِ ابْنِ عُمَرَ رَضِيَ اللّٰهُ عَنْهُمَا، أَنَّ رَسُوْلَ اللّٰهِ صَلَّى اللّٰهُ عَلَيْهِ وَسَلَّمَ قَالَ:
«أُمِرْتُ أَنْ أُقَاتِلَ النَّاسَ حَتَّى يَشْهَدُوا أَنْ لَا إِلٰهَ إِلَّا اللّٰهُ وَأَنَّ مُحَمَّدًا
رَسُوْلُ اللّٰهِ، وَيُقِيْمُوا الصَّلَاةَ، وَيُؤْتُوا الزَّكَاةَ؛ فَإِذَا فَعَلُوا ذٰلِكَ عَصَمُوا مِنِّي
دِمَاءَهُمْ وَأَمْوَالَهُمْ إِلَّا بِحَقِّ الْإِسْلَامِ، وَحِسَابُهُمْ عَلَى اللّٰهِ تَعَالَى».

It is related from Ibn ʿUmar ﷺ that the Prophet ﷺ said,

"I have been commanded to fight people until they testify that there is no god but God and that Muḥammad is the Messenger of God, and they establish the prayer and pay zakat. If they do that, they ensure that their blood and property are safe from me, except by the right of Islam; and their reckoning is with God Most High." [Bukhārī 25, Muslim 22]

Commentary

The Prophet ﷺ did not mention fasting or pilgrimage here, though they are pillars of Islam, because people are not to be fought for neglecting them. That is also why he ﷺ did not mention fasting or pilgrimage to

Muʿādh when he sent him to Yemen to preach Islam. By "except by the right of Islam", he was referring to the laws of Islam about fighting certain offenders such as rebels, highway robbers, assailants, and so on.

By "their reckoning is with God Most High" the Prophet ﷺ meant that if anyone who says the Testimony of Faith, prays, and pays zakat is deemed to be a Muslim citizen protected by the law regardless of whether or not he does so with a sincere intention; for only God knows what is in people's hearts.

HADITH 9

NOT ASKING TOO MANY QUESTIONS

عَنْ أَبِي هُرَيْرَةَ عَبْدِ الرَّحْمٰنِ بْنِ صَخْرٍ رَضِيَ اللّٰهُ عَنْهُ قَالَ:
سَمِعْتُ رَسُوْلَ اللّٰهِ صَلَّى اللّٰهُ عَلَيْهِ وَسَلَّمَ يَقُوْلُ: «مَا نَهَيْتُكُمْ عَنْهُ
فَاجْتَنِبُوْهُ، وَمَا أَمَرْتُكُمْ بِهِ فَأْتُوا مِنْهُ مَا اسْتَطَعْتُمْ، فَإِنَّمَا أَهْلَكَ الَّذِينَ مِنْ
قَبْلِكُمْ كَثْرَةُ مَسَائِلِهِمْ وَاخْتِلَافُهُمْ عَلَى أَنْبِيَائِهِمْ».

Abū Hurayra ﷺ reported that he heard the Prophet ﷺ say,

"Whatever I have forbidden you, keep away from it. Whatever I have ordered you to do, do it as best you can. Those who came before you were only ruined by their excessive questioning and their disagreeing with their Prophets." [Bukhārī 7688, Muslim 1337]

Commentary

If you are uninformed about any matter of obligation such as ablutions, prayer, fasting, or transaction law, you are obliged to ask about it, for the Prophet ﷺ said, "Seeking knowledge is obligatory for every Muslim man and woman." Then there are questions asked in order to obtain a deeper understanding of the religion, not for practical purposes alone.

This is a communal obligation for the Muslims, for God says: *Yet the believers ought not go forth altogether. Only a party from each group of them should go forth, that they may become learned in the faith, then warn their folk when they return to them, so that they may be cautious* [Q. 9:122].

But then there is asking about something that God has not obliged anyone to know—neither you nor anyone else. That is the type of question meant in this hadith, for such questions can lead to hardship. The Prophet ﷺ said, "God has been silent about certain things out of mercy for you, so do not ask about them." ʿAlī ؓ related that when God revealed, *To God do mankind owe pilgrimage to the House—those who can make their way there* [Q. 3:97], a man said, "Does that mean every year, Messenger of God?" The Prophet ﷺ turned away from him, but he repeated his question two or three times until finally the Prophet ﷺ replied, "And what if I said 'yes'? By God, if I said 'yes' it would become obligatory, and you would not be able to do it. You ought to leave me be, for those who came before you were only ruined by their excessive questioning and disagreements with their Prophets." God then revealed, *O you who believe, do not ask about things which, if they were disclosed to you, would trouble you* [Q. 5:101]. This of course referred to the era of the Prophet ﷺ, since afterwards the Law was fixed and could no longer be added to. Nevertheless, many early Muslims also discouraged questions about ambiguous verses of the Qur'an.

HADITH 10

The Lawful is Blessed

عَنْ أَبِي هُرَيْرَةَ رَضِيَ اللّٰهُ عَنْهُ قَالَ: قَالَ رَسُوْلُ اللّٰهِ صَلَّى اللّٰهُ عَلَيْهِ وَسَلَّمَ:
«إِنَّ اللّٰهَ طَيِّبٌ لَا يَقْبَلُ إِلَّا طَيِّبًا، وَإِنَّ اللّٰهَ أَمَرَ الْمُؤْمِنِيْنَ بِمَا أَمَرَ
بِهِ الْمُرْسَلِيْنَ فَقَالَ تَعَالَى: «يَا أَيُّهَا الرُّسُلُ كُلُوْا مِنَ الطَّيِّبَاتِ وَاعْمَلُوا
صَالِحًا»، وَقَالَ تَعَالَى: «يَا أَيُّهَا الَّذِيْنَ آمَنُوْا كُلُوْا مِنْ طَيِّبَاتِ مَا رَزَقْنَاكُمْ»
ثُمَّ ذَكَرَ الرَّجُلَ يُطِيْلُ السَّفَرَ أَشْعَثَ أَغْبَرَ يَمُدُّ يَدَيْهِ إِلَى السَّمَاءِ: يَا رَبِّ!
يَا رَبِّ! وَمَطْعَمُهُ حَرَامٌ، وَمَشْرَبُهُ حَرَامٌ، وَمَلْبَسُهُ حَرَامٌ، وَغُذِّيَ بِالْحَرَامِ،
فَأَنَّى يُسْتَجَابُ لَهُ؟».

Abū Hurayra ﵁ reported that the Prophet ﷺ said,

"God is good, and He accepts only what is good. God gave the same command to the believers as to the Messengers in saying, Exalted is He: *O Messengers, eat of the good things and act righteously* [Q. 23:51]. He also said, Exalted is He: *O you who believe, eat of the good things We have provided you* [Q. 2:172]." He ﷺ then described a man on a long journey, disheveled and dusty, who raises his hands to the sky: "My Lord, my Lord!"—yet his food is unlawful, his drink is unlawful, his clothing is unlawful, and he is nourished with the unlawful. How, then, could his prayer be answered? [Muslim 65]

Commentary

The meaning of "good" is free from defects and blemishes. ʿĀʾisha ﵂ related that the Prophet ﷺ said, "Dear God, I ask You by Your pure and purifying Name, Your good and blessed Name most beloved to You, by which when You are called You answer, and when You are asked You give, and when You are entreated for mercy You show mercy, and when You are begged for relief You grant relief."

"God is good, and accepts only what is good." Nothing unlawful may be given in charity for Him, nor does it please Him when lowly or doubtful things are offered in charity merely to get rid of them. He says, *O you who believe, spend of the good things you have earned and of what We have produced for you from the earth; and do not seek the bad part of it to spend, though you would never take it yourselves save with disdain* [Q. 2:267]. The same applies to actions: He accepts only those deeds that are good and sincere, untainted with ostentation and self-satisfaction.

The hadith shows that you will be rewarded for eating if you intend thereby to gain strength for worship or to keep yourself alive, since that too is an obligation, but not if you eat merely to satiate your appetite.

HADITH 11

Scrupulousness

عَنْ أَبِيْ مُحَمَّدٍ الْحَسَنِ بْنِ عَلِيٍّ بْنِ أَبِيْ طَالِبٍ سِبْطِ رَسُوْلِ اللّٰهِ صَلَّى اللّٰهُ عَلَيْهِ وَسَلَّمَ وَرَيْحَانَتِهِ رَضِيَ اللّٰهُ عَنْهُمَا، قَالَ: حَفِظْتُ مِنْ رَسُوْلِ اللّٰهِ صَلَّى اللّٰهُ عَلَيْهِ وَسَلَّمَ:

«دَعْ مَا يَرِيْبُكَ إِلَى مَا لَا يَرِيْبُكَ».

Al-Ḥasan ibn ʿAlī ibn Abī Ṭālib ﵄, the grandson and the delight of God's Messenger, said: I have memorized this from the Messenger of God ﷺ:

"Leave what makes you doubtful for what does not." [Tirmidhī 2518, Nasāʾī 5711]

Commentary

The God-fearing person avoids consuming things that are doubtful, just as he avoids things that are unlawful. Leave aside doubtful things, and seek things that make your heart tranquil and set your soul at ease.

HADITH 12

Minding One's Own Business

عَنْ أَبِي هُرَيْرَةَ رَضِيَ اللّٰهُ عَنْهُ قَالَ: قَالَ رَسُوْلُ اللّٰهِ صَلَّى اللّٰهُ عَلَيْهِ وَسَلَّمَ:

«مِنْ حُسْنِ إِسْلَامِ الْمَرْءِ تَرْكُهُ مَا لَا يَعْنِيْهِ».

Abū Hurayra ﵁ reported that the Prophet ﷺ said,

"Part of being a good Muslim is to mind one's own business." [Tirmidhī 2318]

Commentary

This means keeping out of anything that does not concern you, whether it be religious or worldly, and whether deeds or words. One of the pieces of advice which the Prophet ﷺ gave to Abū Dharr ﵁ at the latter's request was "It is evil enough for a person to be negligent about his own affairs but concern himself with what is none of his business."

HADITH 13

Love for Others What You Love for Yourself

عَنْ أَبِي حَمْزَةَ أَنَسِ بْنِ مَالِكٍ رَضِيَ اللّٰهُ عَنْهُ خَادِمِ رَسُوْلِ اللّٰهِ صَلَّى اللّٰهُ
عَلَيْهِ وَسَلَّمَ عَنِ النَّبِيِّ صَلَّى اللّٰهُ عَلَيْهِ وَسَلَّمَ قَالَ:
«لَا يُؤْمِنُ أَحَدُكُمْ حَتَّى يُحِبَّ لِأَخِيْهِ مَا يُحِبُّ لِنَفْسِهِ».

Anas ibn Mālik ؓ, the servant of the Messenger of God ﷺ, reported that the Prophet ﷺ said,

"None of you is a true believer until he loves for his brother what he loves for himself." [Bukhārī 13, Muslim 45]

Commentary

This should be understood as referring to the universal brotherhood of man, which includes both Muslims and non-Muslims. The Muslim must love for his non-Muslim brother what he loves for himself, which is that he embrace Islam and hold to it, just as you would wish for your Muslim brother to hold to his Islam. This is why it is recommended to pray that non-Muslims be guided.

The hadith means that your faith is not complete until you love for your brother what you love for yourself. "Love" here means the desire for goodness and benefit. It means religious love, not ordinary human love, for it is sometimes human nature to feel resentful when other people do well and to be envious. But envy is a hateful and unlawful vice. You must fight your human nature and pray for your brother, and share the same hopes for him that you have for yourself. Otherwise, you will stray into envy and resentment of God's decree. God says, *Is it they who apportion the mercy of your Lord? It is We who have apportioned...* [Q. 43:32]. You must minister to your soul and guide it towards contentment with God's decree by praying for others, even your enemies.

HADITH 14

The Sanctity of Muslim Life

عَنِ ابْنِ مَسْعُوْدٍ رَضِيَ اللّٰهُ عَنْهُ قَالَ: قَالَ رَسُوْلُ اللّٰهِ صَلَّى اللّٰهُ عَلَيْهِ وَسَلَّمَ:
«لَا يَحِلُّ دَمُ امْرِئٍ مُسْلِمٍ [يَشْهَدُ أَنْ لَا إِلٰهَ إِلَّا اللّٰهُ، وَأَنِّيْ رَسُوْلُ اللّٰهِ]
إِلَّا بِإِحْدَى ثَلَاثٍ: الثَّيِّبُ الزَّانِي، وَالنَّفْسُ بِالنَّفْسِ، وَالتَّارِكُ لِدِيْنِهِ الْمُفَارِقُ
لِلْجَمَاعَةِ».

Ibn Masʿūd ﵁ reported that the Prophet ﷺ said,

"The blood of every Muslim is inviolable if he testifies that there is no god but God and that I am the Messenger of God, except in three situations: when a married person commits adultery, or when taking a life for a life, or when someone renounces his religion and separates from the Community." [Bukhārī 6878, Muslim 1676]

Commentary

"A married person" (*thayyib*) means someone who has ever been married, even if he is no longer married at the time when he commits adultery. Renouncing religion here means apostatizing from Islam (may God protect us). Jews and Christians converting to each other's religion are not included, since they are not separating from the Community in that sense.

HADITH 15

VIRTUE AND GENEROSITY

عَنْ أَبِي هُرَيْرَةَ رَضِيَ اللّٰهُ عَنْهُ أَنَّ رَسُولَ اللّٰهِ صَلَّى اللّٰهُ عَلَيْهِ وَسَلَّمَ قَالَ:
«مَنْ كَانَ يُؤْمِنُ بِاللّٰهِ وَالْيَوْمِ الْآخِرِ فَلْيَقُلْ خَيْرًا أَوْ لِيَصْمُتْ، وَمَنْ كَانَ
يُؤْمِنُ بِاللّٰهِ وَالْيَوْمِ الْآخِرِ فَلْيُكْرِمْ جَارَهُ، وَمَنْ كَانَ يُؤْمِنُ بِاللّٰهِ وَالْيَوْمِ الْآخِرِ
فَلْيُكْرِمْ ضَيْفَهُ».

Abū Hurayra 🙵 reported that the Prophet 🙵 said,

"He who believes in God and His Messenger should say what is good, or remain silent. He who believes in God and His Messenger should be generous to his neighbor. He who believes in God and His Messenger should be generous to his guest." [Bukhārī 6018, Muslim 47]

Commentary

Imam al-Shāfiʿī said, "This means that you should take a moment to think before speaking, and only speak if you are certain it will not cause any harm."

The great Mālikī scholar of the Maghrib Abū Muḥammad Ibn Abī Zayd said that all of good character is summed up in four hadiths: "He who believes in God and His Messenger should say what is good, or remain silent," "None of you is a true believer until he loves for his brother what he loves for himself," "Part of being a good Muslim is to mind one's own business," and "Do not become angry."

Abū Nuʿaym says in *Ḥilyat al-Awliyāʾ* that you should treat your words like money, and only spend them when you need to. He also said, "If you had to pay for the paper on which the recording angels write your words and deeds, you would talk a lot less!"

The Prophet ﷺ reportedly said, "Nine-tenths of wellbeing lie in being silent except for the remembrance of God." ʿAlī ﵁ said, "A slip of the foot may cause you an injury that soon heals; a slip of the tongue may cost you your life."

Regarding generosity towards neighbors and guests, the Prophet ﷺ said, "Gabriel emphasized to me the importance of honoring one's neighbor so many times that I almost thought he would make the neighbor an heir." Honoring guests is an important part of Islamic ethics and is the character of the Prophets and righteous. Al-Layth [ibn Saʿd, the great jurist]considered offering a night's hospitality to be obligatory. Some scholars hold that the obligation of hospitality falls not only on country people but also on townspeople.

HADITH 16

Do Not Get Angry

عَنْ أَبِي هُرَيْرَةَ رَضِيَ اللّٰهُ عَنْهُ أَنَّ رَجُلًا قَالَ لِلنَّبِيِّ صَلَّى اللّٰهُ عَلَيْهِ وَسَلَّمَ
أَوْصِنِي. قَالَ:

«لَا تَغْضَبْ»، فَرَدَّدَ مِرَارًا، قَالَ: «لَا تَغْضَبْ».

Abū Hurayra ؓ reported that a man said to the Prophet ﷺ, "Give me some parting advice." He replied, "Do not get angry." He asked him again and again, and each time he answered, "Do not get angry." [Bukhārī 6116]

Commentary

Anger is part of human nature, and no one can prevent it from arising, but you can prevent yourself from acting upon it. The Prophet ﷺ said, "Beware of anger, for it is a firebrand kindled in the human heart. Consider how when you become angry your eyes redden and your veins swell up. If you ever feel this then lie down or press yourself to the ground." He ﷺ also said, "Anger is from Satan, and Satan was created from fire; and only water puts out fire. So if you get angry, perform ablution." He ﷺ also said, "If you get angry, sit down if you are standing. If the anger does not go away then lie down."

HADITH 17

EXCELLENCE IN ALL THINGS

عَنْ أَبِيْ يَعْلَى شَدَّادِ بْنِ أَوْسٍ رَضِيَ اللّٰهُ عَنْهُ عَنْ رَسُوْلِ اللّٰهِ صَلَّى اللّٰهُ عَلَيْهِ وَسَلَّمَ قَالَ:

«إِنَّ اللّٰهَ كَتَبَ الْإِحْسَانَ عَلَى كُلِّ شَيْءٍ، فَإِذَا قَتَلْتُمْ فَأَحْسِنُوا الْقِتْلَةَ، وَإِذَا ذَبَحْتُمْ فَأَحْسِنُوا الذِّبْحَةَ، وَلْيُحِدَّ أَحَدُكُمْ شَفْرَتَهُ، وَلْيُرِحْ ذَبِيحَتَهُ».

Shaddād ibn Aws ﵁ related that the Prophet ﷺ said:

"God has prescribed excellence for all things. When you kill, kill well; and when you slaughter, slaughter well. One should sharpen one's blade, and put the slaughtered animal at ease." [Muslim 1955]

Commentary

An execution must be performed with the proper instrument and not with any old tool. Likewise, when slaughtering an animal a sharp blade must be used. The comfort of the animal must be ensured; no part may be cut from it before it is dead, nor should the knife be sharpened in front of it. Water should be provided to it beforehand. Animals that are nursing their infants should not be slaughtered until the infants are weaned. It is also said that one animal should not be slaughtered in front of another. When milking an animal, one should make sure one's fingernails are trimmed, and avoid milking it completely dry.

HADITH 18

Good Character

عَنْ أَبِي ذَرٍّ جُنْدُبِ بْنِ جُنَادَةَ، وَأَبِي عَبْدِ الرَّحْمٰنِ مُعَاذِ بْنِ جَبَلٍ رَضِيَ اللّٰهُ عَنْهُمَا، عَنْ رَسُوْلِ اللّٰهِ صَلَّى اللّٰهُ عَلَيْهِ وَسَلَّمَ قَالَ:

«اتَّقِ اللّٰهَ حَيْثُمَا كُنْتَ، وَأَتْبِعِ السَّيِّئَةَ الْحَسَنَةَ تَمْحُهَا، وَخَالِقِ النَّاسَ بِخُلُقٍ حَسَنٍ».

Abū Dharr and Muʿādh ibn Jabal ﵄ both related that the Prophet ﷺ said,

"Be conscious of God wherever you may be. Follow a bad deed with a good one to erase it. Treat people with good character." [Tirmidhī 1987]

Commentary

"Be conscious of God wherever you may be." That is, be conscious of God in private just as you are in public, and at all places and times. This is helped by calling to mind that He can always see you; as He says, Exalted is He, *No secret conversation takes place among three but He is their fourth* [Q. 58:7].

"Follow a bad deed with a good one to erase it." If you commit a sin, ask God to forgive you for it, and do a good deed to erase it. A single good deed erases many bad deeds, for the Prophet ﷺ said, "Say *Allāhu Akbar* ten times, *al-ḥamdu li-Llāh* ten times, and *subḥānaLlāh* ten times after each prayer. That makes one hundred and fifty [per day] uttered with the tongue, but one thousand and five hundred in the Scale. Who among you commits one thousand and five hundred sins in a single day?"

The hadith shows the importance of holding oneself to account. The Prophet ﷺ said, "Hold yourselves to account before you are held to account." God says, *O you who believe, be conscious of God, and let every soul consider what it has sent ahead for tomorrow* [Q. 59:18].

"Treat people with good character." The term "good character" means treating people kindly and avoiding harming them. The Prophet ﷺ said, "You will never have enough wealth to give to everyone, but you can give them all a cheerful face and good character." He ﷺ also said, "The best of you are those with the best character." When a man asked him what was the best deed of all he ﷺ replied, "Good character." Abū Hurayra ؓ related that the Messenger of God ﷺ said, "The believers with the most complete faith are those with the best character, and the best of them are those who are best to their womenfolk." He ﷺ also said, "God has chosen Islam for you, so honor it with good character and generosity, for without them it is incomplete."

HADITH 19

God-Consciousness

عَنْ عَبْدِ اللّٰهِ بْنِ عَبَّاسٍ رَضِيَ اللّٰهُ عَنْهُمَا قَالَ:

«كُنْتُ خَلْفَ رَسُوْلِ اللّٰهِ صَلَّى اللّٰهُ عَلَيْهِ وَسَلَّمَ يَوْمًا، فَقَالَ: يَا غُلَامُ! إِنِّي أُعَلِّمُكَ كَلِمَاتٍ: اِحْفَظِ اللّٰهَ يَحْفَظْكَ، اِحْفَظِ اللّٰهَ تَجِدْهُ تُجَاهَكَ، إِذَا سَأَلْتَ فَاسْأَلِ اللّٰهَ، وَإِذَا اسْتَعَنْتَ فَاسْتَعِنْ بِاللّٰهِ، وَاعْلَمْ أَنَّ الْأُمَّةَ لَوِ اجْتَمَعَتْ عَلَى أَنْ يَنْفَعُوْكَ بِشَيْءٍ لَمْ يَنْفَعُوْكَ إِلَّا بِشَيْءٍ قَدْ كَتَبَهُ اللّٰهُ لَكَ، وَإِنِ اجْتَمَعُوْا عَلَى أَنْ يَضُرُّوكَ بِشَيْءٍ لَمْ يَضُرُّوكَ إِلَّا بِشَيْءٍ قَدْ كَتَبَهُ اللّٰهُ عَلَيْكَ؛ رُفِعَتِ الْأَقْلَامُ، وَجَفَّتِ الصُّحُفُ».

وَفِي رِوَايَةِ غَيْرِ التِّرْمِذِيِّ:

«اِحْفَظِ اللّٰهَ تَجِدْهُ أَمَامَكَ، تَعَرَّفْ إِلَى اللّٰهِ فِي الرَّخَاءِ يَعْرِفْكَ فِي الشِّدَّةِ، وَاعْلَمْ أَنَّ مَا أَخْطَأَكَ لَمْ يَكُنْ لِيُصِيبَكَ، وَمَا أَصَابَكَ لَمْ يَكُنْ لِيُخْطِئَكَ، وَاعْلَمْ أَنَّ النَّصرَ مَعَ الصَّبْرِ، وَأَنَّ الْفَرَجَ مَعَ الْكَرْبِ، وَأَنَّ مَعَ الْعُسْرِ يُسْرًا».

Ibn ʿAbbās 🙵 reported:

"One day I was sitting behind the Prophet 🙵 and he said: "Son, I shall teach you some words to live by. Watch over God, and He will watch over you. Watch over God, and you will find Him in front of you. When you ask, ask of God. When you seek help, seek it from God. Know that if the whole world were to work together to benefit you, they could not benefit you in the least unless God had destined it for you; and if they worked together to harm you, they could not harm you in the least unless God had destined it for you. The pens have been lifted, and the pages have dried.""

Another narration, not that of Tirmidhī, has:

"Watch over God, and you will find Him in front of you. Make yourself known to God in times of comfort, and He will know you in times of hardship. Know that nothing that misses you was ever going to hit you, and nothing that hits you was ever going to miss you. Know that victory comes with patience, and relief comes with suffering, and with difficulty comes ease." [Tirmidhī 2516]

Commentary
If you watch over God by observing His commandments and prohibitions, He will watch over you in your worldly and otherworldly affairs. God says, *Whoever does right, whether male or female, and is a believer, We shall quicken them with a goodly life* [Q. 16:97]. When people suffer tribulations and misfortunes, it is because God's commandments are being disregarded. God says, *Whatever misfortune may befall you is for what your own hands have earned* [Q. 43:20].

"Watch over God, and you will find Him in front of you." Or, as he 🙵 also said, "Make yourself known to God in times of comfort, and He will know you in times of hardship." God says in His Book that righteous action helps in difficult times and bring salvation, while unrighteous action leads to greater difficulty. He says of Jonah 🙵, *Had he not been one of those who glorify, he would have tarried in its belly till the Day they are raised* [Q. 37:143–144].

"When you ask, ask of God." Attach your innermost heart to God and rely on Him in all things. If you need something that can only come from God, ask Him for it. If you need something that He normally sends through human means, ask Him to make the hearts of those humans incline towards you. Do not ask Him to free you of need for other people, for when the Prophet ﷺ heard ʿAlī pray for that, he said, "Do not say that, for people need one another. But ask God to free you of need for evil people."

"Know that if the whole world were to work together. . ." Everyone hopes for good for those he loves, and worries about evil from those he fears. Therefore God tells us not to put our hopes in others, saying: *If God afflicts you with harm, none can remove it but Him; and if He desires good for you, none can repel His grace* [Q. 10:107]. Yet this does not mean that we should be reckless and blindly trust for the best, for we must always seek the means of safety and flee from the means of harm. God says, *Do not hurl yourselves into ruin with your own hands* [Q. 2:195].

"Know that help comes with patience, and relief comes with suffering, and with difficulty comes ease." The Prophet ﷺ said, "Do not hope to meet the enemy in battle; ask God for wellbeing. But if you must meet them, be steadfast and do not flee, for God is with the steadfast." It is the way of God to send relief after suffering, and ease with difficulty. God says, *For truly with hardship comes ease; truly with hardship comes ease* [Q. 94:5–6]. The Prophet ﷺ said of this, "One hardship could not defeat two eases." This is because in the verse the word *al-ʿusr*, "hardship", has the definite article while *yusr*, "ease", does not; and in the customary usage of the Arabs, when a definite noun is repeated both instances are taken to refer to the same thing, while a repeated indefinite noun is taken as two things. Hence there are two eases and there is only one hardship.

HADITH 20

SHAME

عَنْ أَبِيْ مَسْعُوْدٍ عُقْبَةَ بْنِ عَمْرٍو الأَنْصَارِيِّ الْبَدْرِيِّ رَضِيَ اللّٰهُ عَنْهُ قَالَ:
قَالَ رَسُوْلُ اللهِ صَلَّى اللّٰهُ عَلَيْهِ وَسَلَّمَ:
«إِنَّ مِمَّا أَدْرَكَ النَّاسُ مِنْ كَلَامِ النُّبُوَّةِ الْأُوْلَى: إِذَا لَمْ تَسْتَحِ فَاصْنَعْ مَا شِئْتَ».

ʿUqba ibn ʿAmr al-Anṣārī ﷺ reported that the Prophet ﷺ said,

"One of the first teachings of Prophethood to reach mankind was: If you do not feel ashamed, do as you please." [Bukhārī 3483]

Commentary

This means that if you want to do something and there is no reason why you should feel ashamed to do it—before God, not before your fellow man—then you may do it. Otherwise, you should not. The whole of Islam revolves around this hadith. Alternatively, the hadith can be interpreted as meaning that if a person does not feel shame before God or awareness of His presence he may as well allow himself to do as he pleases. This would cast the hadith as a warning rather than a permission. It is in that sense that God says, *Do as you wish; truly He sees what you do* [Q. 41:40], and that He said to Satan, '*Stir up whomever of them you can with your voice*' [Q. 17:64].

HADITH 21

Uprightness

عَنْ أَبِيْ عَمْرٍو وَقِيْلَ: أَبِيْ عَمْرَةَ سُفْيَانَ بْنِ عَبْدِ اللّٰهِ رَضِيَ اللّٰهُ عَنْهُ قَالَ:

«قُلْتُ: يَا رَسُوْلَ اللّٰهِ! قُلْ لِيْ فِي الْإِسْلَامِ قَوْلًا لَا أَسْأَلُ عَنْهُ أَحَدًا

غَيْرَكَ؛ قَالَ: قُلْ: آمَنْتُ بِاللّٰهِ ثُمَّ اسْتَقِمْ».

Sufyān ibn ʿAbd Allāh ﷺ reported that he said,

"Messenger of God, tell me something about Islam that I could ask of no one but you." The Prophet ﷺ replied, "Say, 'I believe in God,' then be upright." [Muslim 38]

Commentary

Uprightness (*istiqāma*) means holding to the path by fulfilling your obligations and avoiding what is forbidden you. God says, *So be upright as you have been commanded, with those who repent alongside you* [Q. 11:112]; and says, *Truly those who say, 'Our Lord is God' and then are upright, the angels descend upon them saying, 'Fear not, nor grieve, but rejoice in the Garden that you are promised. We are your protectors in the present life and in the Hereafter'* [Q. 41:30–31]. The angels descend upon them at the moment of death and give them these glad tidings. They ask what will become of the children they have left behind, and the angels reassure them on that account.

HADITH 22

The Key to Paradise

عَنْ أَبِي عَبْدِ اللّٰهِ جَابِرِ بْنِ عَبْدِ اللّٰهِ الْأَنْصَارِيِّ رَضِيَ اللّٰهُ عَنْهُمَا:

«أَنَّ رَجُلًا سَأَلَ رَسُوْلَ اللّٰهِ صَلَّى اللّٰهُ عَلَيْهِ وَسَلَّمَ فَقَالَ: أَرَأَيْتَ إِذَا صَلَّيْتُ الْمَكْتُوبَاتِ، وَصُمْتُ رَمَضَانَ، وَأَحْلَلْتُ الْحَلَالَ، وَحَرَّمْتُ الْحَرَامَ، وَلَمْ أَزِدْ عَلَى ذَلِكَ شَيْئًا؛ أَأَدْخُلُ الْجَنَّةَ؟ قَالَ: نَعَمْ».

Jābir ibn ʿAbd Allāh ﷺ related that a man asked the Prophet ﷺ,

"What if I perform the obligatory prayers, fast Ramaḍān, treat the lawful as lawful and the forbidden as forbidden, and do no more than that—will I go to Paradise?" He replied, "Yes." [Muslim 15]

Commentary

To treat the lawful as lawful means to believe in its lawfulness and fulfill its obligations. To treat the unlawful as unlawful means to believe in its unlawfulness and abstain from it.

Ibn Daqīq al-ʿĪd: The Prophet ﷺ did not mention any voluntary deeds to the questioner, which indicates that it is permissible to omit them. Nevertheless, to neglect them is to pass up a tremendous opportunity for spiritual advancement and merit, and to persistently neglect the regular voluntary practices of the Prophet ﷺ entirely is a blemish on your religion and your character. The Companions ﷺ and the early generations after them did not stress the distinction between obligatory and voluntary deeds, but simply followed the Sunna. The distinction did not come to be emphasized until the imams of jurisprudence resorted to it in order to explain which acts must be made up for and which need not be, and which acts it is sinful to miss. The Prophet ﷺ did not want to discourage the questioner by reminding him of voluntary deeds, since he was a new convert and that might have been too much for him. He knew that once he became more firmly rooted in Islam and God expanded his heart, his aspiration would rise to something greater.

HADITH 23

Prophetic Counsels

عَنْ أَبِيْ مَالِكٍ الْحَارِثِ بْنِ عَاصِمٍ الْأَشْعَرِيِّ رَضِيَ اللّٰهُ عَنْهُ قَالَ: قَالَ رَسُوْلُ اللّٰهِ صَلَّى اللّٰهُ عَلَيْهِ وَسَلَّمَ:

«الطَّهُوْرُ شَطْرُ الإِيْمَانِ، وَالْحَمْدُ لِلّٰهِ تَمْلَأُ الْمِيْزَانَ، وَسُبْحَانَ اللّٰهِ وَالْحَمْدُ لِلّٰهِ تَمْلَآنِ - أَوْ: تَمْلَأُ - مَا بَيْنَ السَّمَاءِ وَالْأَرْضِ، وَالصَّلَاةُ نُوْرٌ، وَالصَّدَقَةُ بُرْهَانٌ، وَالصَّبْرُ ضِيَاءٌ، وَالْقُرْآنُ حُجَّةٌ لَكَ أَوْ عَلَيْكَ، كُلُّ النَّاسِ يَغْدُوْ، فَبَائِعٌ نَفْسَهُ فَمُعْتِقُهَا أَوْ مُوبِقُهَا».

Al-Ḥārith ibn ʿĀṣim ﵁ reported that the Messenger of God ﷺ said:

"Purity is half of faith. 'Praise be to God' (*al-ḥamdu li-Llāh*) fills the scale. 'Glory be to God and praise be to God' (*subḥānaLlāhi wal-ḥamdu li-Llāh*) fills everything between heaven and earth. Prayer is light. Charity is proof. Patience is illumination. The Qurʾān is an argument either for you or against you. All those who live to see another day sell their souls—either into freedom or into ruin."

[Muslim 15]

Commentary

Al-Ghazālī explained "purity" to mean the heart's purity from rancor, envy, and all its other ailments, for faith is incomplete without this purity. Someone said that when you purify your heart, perform ablutions, and then pray, you enter prayer with two purifications; but if you wash your limbs alone, you enter it with only one. God is concerned only with purity of heart: as the Prophet ﷺ said, "God does not look at your forms or your faces; He looks at your hearts."

"Prayer is light" means that its reward is light, as in the hadith, "Tell those who walk to the mosque in the dark that they shall have a perfect light on the Day of Resurrection."

"Charity is proof" of a person's true faith, which is why it is called *ṣadaqa*, "truth." A hypocrite may pray easily but finds it very difficult to give charity.

"Patience is illumination." This means praiseworthy patience, which is to be steadfast in obedience to God and to bear the tribulations and evils of the world with forbearance.

"All those who live to see another day sell their souls—either into freedom, or into ruin." All people pursue some purpose for themselves. Some offer themselves to God by obeying Him, thereby freeing themselves from damnation. Others offer themselves to Satan and caprice by following them, and so fall into ruin. God says, *Truly God has purchased from the believers their lives and their possessions in exchange for Paradise* [Q. 9:111].

HADITH 24

The Blessings of God

عَنْ أَبِي ذَرٍّ الْغِفَارِيِّ رَضِيَ اللّٰهُ عَنْهُ عَنِ النَّبِيِّ صَلَّى اللّٰهُ عَلَيْهِ وَسَلَّمَ فِيْمَا يَرْوِيْهِ عَنْ رَبِّهِ تَبَارَكَ وَتَعَالَى، أَنَّهُ قَالَ:

«يَا عِبَادِيْ: إِنِّي حَرَّمْتُ الظُّلْمَ عَلَى نَفْسِيْ، وَجَعَلْتُهُ بَيْنَكُمْ مُحَرَّمًا؛ فَلَا تَظَالَمُوْا.

يَا عِبَادِيْ! كُلُّكُمْ ضَالٌّ إِلَّا مَنْ هَدَيْتُهُ، فَاسْتَهْدُوْنِيْ أَهْدِكُمْ.

يَا عِبَادِيْ! كُلُّكُمْ جَائِعٌ إِلَّا مَنْ أَطْعَمْتُهُ، فَاسْتَطْعِمُونِيْ أُطْعِمْكُمْ.

يَا عِبَادِيْ! كُلُّكُمْ عَارٍ إِلَّا مَنْ كَسَوْتُهُ، فَاسْتَكْسُونِيْ أَكْسُكُمْ.

يَا عِبَادِيْ! إِنَّكُمْ تُخْطِئُوْنَ بِاللَّيْلِ وَالنَّهَارِ، وَأَنَا أَغْفِرُ الذُّنُوْبَ جَمِيْعًا؛ فَاسْتَغْفِرُونِيْ أَغْفِرْ لَكُمْ.

يَا عِبَادِيْ! إِنَّكُمْ لَنْ تَبْلُغُوْا ضُرِّي فَتَضُرُّونِي، وَلَنْ تَبْلُغُوْا نَفْعِيْ فَتَنْفَعُونِيْ.

يَا عِبَادِيْ! لَوْ أَنَّ أَوَّلَكُمْ وَآخِرَكُمْ وَإِنْسَكُمْ وَجِنَّكُمْ كَانُوْا عَلَى أَتْقَى قَلْبِ رَجُلٍ وَاحِدٍ مِنْكُمْ، مَا زَادَ ذَلِكَ فِي مُلْكِيْ شَيْئًا.

يَا عِبَادِيْ! لَوْ أَنَّ أَوَّلَكُمْ وَآخِرَكُمْ وَإِنْسَكُمْ وَجِنَّكُمْ كَانُوْا عَلَى أَفْجَرِ قَلْبِ رَجُلٍ وَاحِدٍ مِنْكُمْ، مَا نَقَصَ ذَلِكَ مِنْ مُلْكِي شَيْئًا.

يَا عِبَادِيْ! لَوْ أَنَّ أَوَّلَكُمْ وَآخِرَكُمْ وَإِنْسَكُمْ وَجِنَّكُمْ قَامُوْا فِي صَعِيْدٍ وَاحِدٍ، فَسَأَلُوْنِيْ، فَأَعْطَيْتُ كُلَّ وَاحِدٍ مَسْأَلَتَهُ، مَا نَقَصَ ذَلِكَ مِمَّا عِنْدِيْ إِلَّا كَمَا يَنْقُصُ الْمِخْيَطُ إِذَا أُدْخِلَ الْبَحْرَ.

يَا عِبَادِيْ! إِنَّمَا هِيَ أَعْمَالُكُمْ أُحْصِيهَا لَكُمْ، ثُمَّ أُوَفِّيكُمْ إِيَّاهَا؛ فَمَنْ وَجَدَ خَيْرًا فَلْيَحْمَدِ اللّٰهَ، وَمَنْ وَجَدَ غَيْرَ ذَلِكَ فَلَا يَلُوْمَنَّ إِلَّا نَفْسَهُ».

Abū Dharr ﵁ conveyed from the Prophet ﷺ that he related that his Lord, the Mighty and Majestic, says:

"My servants, I have forbidden Myself injustice and made it forbidden among you, so be not unjust.

"My servants, all of you are astray save whom I guide, so seek My guidance and I shall guide you.

"My servants, all of you are hungry save whom I feed, so ask Me for food and I shall feed you.

"My servants, all of you are naked save whom I clothe, so ask Me for clothing and I shall clothe you.

"My servants, you sin by night and day, and I forgive all sins, so ask My forgiveness and I shall forgive you.

"My servants, you could never reach My harm so as to harm Me, nor reach My benefit so as to benefit Me.

"My servants, if all of you from first to last, human to jinn, had hearts as reverent as the most reverent man among you, it would not add to My kingdom in the least.

"My servants, if all of you from first to last, human to jinn, had hearts as wicked as the most wicked man among you, it would not detract from My kingdom in the least.

"My servants, if all of you from first to last, human to jinn, rose up in one place and asked of Me, and I gave each one what he asked, it would take no more of what is Mine than a thread dipped into the sea takes from it.

"My servants, it is nothing but your deeds that I count up for you, then recompense you for in full. Let him who finds good praise God, and let him who finds anything else blame none but himself." [Muslim 2577]

Commentary

It is impossible that God could be unjust, for injustice means to cross the limit and encroach upon the property of another, which is inconceivable for God.

It is also apparent, both from Scripture and from reason, that God is absolutely independent of all things, and unaffected by His creatures. He has no need for creation, nor for any partner. He does not need our obedience, and even if every last one of us were as reverent as could be and obeyed Him totally, it would not affect Him or add anything to His kingdom. Their obedience is due only to His grace and guidance; it is His gift to them, not theirs to Him; and their disobedience does not hurt Him, but only themselves.

HADITH 25

Competing in Virtue

عَنْ أَبِي ذَرٍّ رَضِيَ اللّٰهُ عَنْهُ أَيْضًا:

«أَنَّ نَاسًا مِنْ أَصْحَابِ رَسُوْلِ اللّٰهِ صَلَّى اللّٰهُ عَلَيْهِ وَسَلَّمَ قَالُوْا لِلنَّبِيِّ صَلَّى اللّٰهُ عَلَيْهِ وَسَلَّمَ يَا رَسُولَ اللّٰهِ ذَهَبَ أَهْلُ الدُّثُوْرِ بِالْأُجُوْرِ؛ يُصَلُّوْنَ كَمَا نُصَلِّيْ، وَيَصُوْمُوْنَ كَمَا نَصُوْمُ، وَيَتَصَدَّقُوْنَ بِفُضُوْلِ أَمْوَالِهِمْ. قَالَ: أَوَلَيْسَ قَدْ جَعَلَ اللّٰهُ لَكُمْ مَا تَصَّدَّقُوْنَ؟ إِنَّ بِكُلِّ تَسْبِيحَةٍ صَدَقَةً، وَكُلِّ تَكْبِيرَةٍ صَدَقَةً، وَكُلِّ تَحْمِيْدَةٍ صَدَقَةً، وَكُلِّ تَهْلِيْلَةٍ صَدَقَةً، وَأَمْرٌ بِمَعْرُوْفٍ صَدَقَةٌ، وَنَهْيٌ عَنْ مُنْكَرٍ صَدَقَةٌ، وَفِي بُضْعِ أَحَدِكُمْ صَدَقَةٌ. قَالُوْا: يَا رَسُوْلَ اللّٰهِ أَيَأْتِي أَحَدُنَا شَهْوَتَهُ وَيَكُوْنُ لَهُ فِيهَا أَجْرٌ؟ قَالَ: أَرَأَيْتُمْ لَوْ وَضَعَهَا فِي حَرَامٍ أَكَانَ عَلَيْهِ وِزْرٌ؟ فَكَذَلِكَ إِذَا وَضَعَهَا فِي الْحَلَالِ، كَانَ لَهُ أَجْرٌ».

Abū Dharr ﵁ also reported that,

"Some of the Companions asked the Prophet ﷺ, Messenger of God, the wealthy have carried off the rewards. They pray just as we do, and fast just as we do, and they give their spare wealth in charity."

He ﷺ replied, "But has God not given you the means to give charity, too? Every *subḥānaLlāh* is charity, every *Allāhu Akbar* is charity, every *al-ḥamdu li-Llāh* is charity, and every *lāilāhaillā-Allāh* is charity. Enjoining what is right is charity, and forbidding what is wrong is charity. There is even charity for you in having sex with your wives!"

They said, "Messenger of God, do you mean to say that a man is rewarded for satisfying his lust?"

He replied, "Well, tell me: if he satisfied it in an unlawful way, would he not be guilty of sin? Just so, when he satisfies it lawfully, he is rewarded." [Muslim 1006]

Commentary

Sexual desire has always been something dear to the Prophets and the righteous because of its advantages both worldly and spiritual. It helps with lowering the gaze and breaking the desire for adultery, as well as being the means for procreation and thereby the population of the world and the continuation of the Community until the Day of Resurrection. All desires harden the heart except for this one, which softens it.

HADITH 26

The Many Forms of Charity

عَنْ أَبِي هُرَيْرَةَ رَضِيَ اللّٰهُ عَنْهُ قَالَ: قَالَ رَسُوْلُ اللّٰهِ صَلَّى اللّٰهُ عَلَيْهِ وَسَلَّمَ:
«كُلُّ سُلَامَى مِنَ النَّاسِ عَلَيْهِ صَدَقَةٌ، كُلَّ يَوْمٍ تَطْلُعُ فِيهِ الشَّمْسُ تَعْدِلُ
بَيْنَ اثْنَيْنِ صَدَقَةٌ، وَتُعِينُ الرَّجُلَ فِي دَابَّتِهِ فَتَحْمِلُهُ عَلَيْهَا أَوْ تَرْفَعُ لَهُ عَلَيْهَا
مَتَاعَهُ صَدَقَةٌ، وَالْكَلِمَةُ الطَّيِّبَةُ صَدَقَةٌ، وَبِكُلِّ خُطْوَةٍ تَمْشِيهَا إِلَى الصَّلَاةِ
صَدَقَةٌ، وَتُمِيطُ الْأَذَى عَنِ الطَّرِيْقِ صَدَقَةٌ».

Abū Dharr reported that the Messenger of God ﷺ said,

"Charity is due upon every joint in every person's body, on every day the sun rises. To put things right between two people is charity. To help a man with his mount and load his baggage onto it is charity. A good word is charity. Every step you take towards the prayer is charity. To remove anything harmful from a pathway is charity." [Bukhārī 2989, Muslim 1009]

Commentary

It is said that there are three hundred and sixty joints in the human body, on each of which charity is owed every day. Each righteous deed is an act of charity, as described in the hadith. If you fulfill this at the start of the day, you pay the zakat on your body, and you may keep the rest of your good deeds that day for yourself.

HADITH 27

PIETY AND SIN

عَنِ النَّوَّاسِ بْنِ سَمْعَانَ رَضِيَ اللّٰهُ عَنْهُ عَنِ النَّبِيِّ صَلَّى اللّٰهُ عَلَيْهِ وَسَلَّمَ قَالَ: «الْبِرُّ حُسْنُ الْخُلُقِ، وَالْإِثْمُ مَا حَاكَ فِي صَدْرِكَ، وَكَرِهْتَ أَنْ يَطَّلِعَ عَلَيْهِ النَّاسُ».

وَعَنْ وَابِصَةَ بْنِ مَعْبَدٍ رَضِيَ اللّٰهُ عَنْهُ قَالَ: أَتَيْتُ رَسُوْلَ اللّٰهِ صَلَّى اللّٰهُ عَلَيْهِ وَسَلَّمَ فَقَالَ:

«جِئْتَ تَسْأَلُ عَنِ الْبِرِّ؟ قُلْتُ: نَعَمْ. فقَالَ: اِسْتَفْتِ قَلْبَكَ، اَلْبِرُّ مَا اطْمَأَنَّتْ إِلَيْهِ النَّفْسُ، وَاطْمَأَنَّ إِلَيْهِ الْقَلْبُ، وَالْإِثْمُ مَا حَاكَ فِي النَّفْسِ وَتَرَدَّدَ فِي الصَّدْرِ، وَإِنْ أَفْتَاكَ النَّاسُ وَأَفْتَوْكَ».

Al-Nawwās ibn Samʿān ﷺ reported that the Prophet ﷺ said,

"Piety is good character. Sin is that which disturbs your conscience and which you would hate for people to find out."

Wābiṣa ibn Maʿbad related that the Prophet ﷺ said to him,

"Have you come to ask about piety?" He replied, "Yes." He said, "Consult your heart. Piety is what makes the soul tranquil and the heart tranquil. Sin is what makes the soul feel uneasy and the heart waver, no matter what people tell you." [Muslim 2553]

Commentary

Ibn ʿUmar said, "Piety is a simple matter: a cheerful face and a gentle tongue." God sums up the different forms of piety in His Words, *Piety is not that you turn your faces to the East or the West. Piety is the one who believes in God and the Last Day, the Angels, the Books, and the Prophets; and who gives of his possessions, however cherished, to kinsfolk, and orphans, and the needy, and travelers, and beggars, and in order to free slaves; and who observes the prayer and pays the alms; and those who fulfil their covenants when they make them; and those who are patient in misfortune, hardship, and times of peril. Such are the sincere ones. Such are the reverent* [Q. 2:177].

The hadith shows that you must consult your heart before you do anything, and only do it if your soul feels at ease with it. It is said that Adam said to his children, "If you are about to do something and your heart feels uneasy, do not do it. When I was about to eat from the Tree, my heart felt uneasy. Consider the consequences of your actions; for had I considered the consequence of eating from the Tree, I would not have done it."

He said, "and which you would hate for people to find out" because people will look down on you for doing something doubtful, never mind something unlawful. This also applies to taking something that belongs to someone else: if you are certain that they would not mind, it is lawful; but otherwise it is not.

"Sin is what makes the soul feel uneasy and the heart waver, no matter what people tell you." Suppose, for instance, you receive a gift from someone whose income comes mostly from unlawful sources, which makes you hesitant about accepting it. You ask the mufti and he tells you that it is lawful, but the fatwa does not dispel your doubts. In such cases the right thing to do is to abstain from taking it, out of scrupulousness. God knows best.

HADITH 28

Holding to the Sunna

عَنْ أَبِيْ نَجِيْحِ الْعِرْبَاضِ بْنِ سَارِيَةَ رَضِيَ اللّٰهُ عَنْهُ قَالَ:

«وَعَظَنَا رَسُوْلُ اللّٰهِ صَلَّى اللّٰهُ عَلَيْهِ وَسَلَّمَ مَوْعِظَةً وَجِلَتْ مِنْهَا الْقُلُوْبُ، وَذَرَفَتْ مِنْهَا الْعُيُوْنُ، فَقُلْنَا: يَا رَسُوْلَ اللّٰهِ! كَأَنَّهَا مَوْعِظَةُ مُوَدِّعٍ فَأَوْصِنَا، قَالَ: أُوْصِيْكُمْ بِتَقْوَى اللّٰهِ، وَالسَّمْعِ وَالطَّاعَةِ وَإِنْ تَأَمَّرَ عَلَيْكُمْ عَبْدٌ، فَإِنَّهُ مَنْ يَعِشْ مِنْكُمْ فَسَيَرَى اخْتِلَافًا كَثِيْرًا، فَعَلَيْكُمْ بِسُنَّتِي وَسُنَّةِ الْخُلَفَاءِ الرَّاشِدِينَ الْمَهْدِيِّيْنَ، عَضُّوا عَلَيْهَا بِالنَّوَاجِذِ، وَإِيَّاكُمْ وَمُحْدَثَاتِ الْأُمُوْرِ؛ فَإِنَّ كُلَّ بِدْعَةٍ ضَلَالَةٌ».

ʿIrbāḍ ibn Sāriya رضي الله عنه said,

"The Messenger of God ﷺ gave us a sermon that made our hearts tremble and brought tears to our eyes. We said, 'Messenger of God, that seemed like a farewell speech. Give us one last counsel.'

"He ﷺ replied, 'I counsel you to be conscious of God, and to hear and obey even if your commander is a slave. Those of you who live will witness much conflict. You must adhere to my Sunna and the Sunna of the righteous, rightly-guided Successors. Hold onto it with your very teeth! Beware of newly invented things, for every innovation is misguidance.'" [Abū Dāwūd 4607, Tirmidhī 266]

Commentary

The Prophet ﷺ counseled us that when times of discord arise, we must hold fast to his Sunna by following it and disregarding the opinions of those who are on the side of caprice and innovation. By "the righteous, rightly-guided Successors" he meant the Four: Abū Bakr, ʿUmar, ʿUthmān, and ʿAlī, may God be pleased with them.

HADITH 29

The Path to Salvation

عَنْ مُعَاذِ بْنِ جَبَلٍ رَضِيَ اللّٰهُ عَنْهُ قَالَ:

قُلْتُ يَا رَسُوْلَ اللّٰهِ! أَخْبِرْنِيْ بِعَمَلٍ يُدْخِلُنِي الْجَنَّةَ وَيُبَاعِدُنِيْ مِنَ النَّارِ، قَالَ: «لَقَدْ سَأَلْتَ عَنْ عَظِيمٍ، وَإِنَّهُ لَيَسِيْرٌ عَلَى مَنْ يَسَّرَهُ اللّٰهُ عَلَيْهِ: تَعْبُدُ اللّٰهَ لَا تُشْرِكْ بِهِ شَيْئًا، وَتُقِيْمُ الصَّلَاةَ، وَتُؤْتِي الزَّكَاةَ، وَتَصُوْمُ رَمَضَانَ، وَتَحُجُّ الْبَيْتَ، ثُمَّ قَالَ: أَلَا أَدُلُّكَ عَلَى أَبْوَابِ الْخَيْرِ؟ الصَّوْمُ جُنَّةٌ، وَالصَّدَقَةُ تُطْفِئُ الْخَطِيْئَةَ كَمَا يُطْفِئُ الْمَاءُ النَّارَ، وَصَلَاةُ الرَّجُلِ فِي جَوْفِ اللَّيْلِ، ثُمَّ تَلَا: «تَتَجَافَى جُنُوْبُهُمْ عَنِ الْمَضَاجِعِ» حَتَّى بَلَغَ «يَعْمَلُونَ»، [٣٢ سورة السجدة / الآيتان: ١٦ و١٧] ثُمَّ قَالَ: أَلَا أُخْبِرُك بِرَأْسِ الْأَمْرِ وَعَمُودِهِ وَذِرْوَةِ سَنَامِهِ؟ قُلْتُ: بَلَى يَا رَسُولَ اللّٰهِ. قَالَ: رَأْسُ الْأَمْرِ الْإِسْلَامُ، وَعَمُوْدُهُ الصَّلَاةُ، وَذِرْوَةُ سَنَامِهِ الْجِهَادُ، ثُمَّ قَالَ: أَلَا أُخْبِرُك بِمَلَاكِ ذَلِكَ

كُلِّهِ؟ فقُلْتُ: بَلَى يَا رَسُوْلَ اللهِ! فَأَخَذَ بِلِسَانِهِ وَقَالَ: كُفَّ عَلَيْكَ هَذَا. قُلْتُ:
يَا نَبِيَّ اللهِ وَإِنَّا لَمُؤَاخَذُوْنَ بِمَا نَتَكَلَّمُ بِهِ؟ فَقَالَ: ثَكِلَتْكَ أُمُّكَ وَهَلْ يَكُبُّ
النَّاسَ عَلَى وُجُوهِهِمْ - أَوْ قَالَ عَلَى مَنَاخِرِهِمْ - إِلَّا حَصَائِدُ أَلْسِنَتِهِمْ؟!».

It is related from Muʿādh ibn Jabal ؓ that,

"I asked God's Messenger ﷺ, Tell me of a deed that will take me to Paradise and keep me far from Hell." He replied, "You have asked about something momentous, and yet it is easy for those for whom God makes it easy. Worship God and associate nothing with Him, observe prayer, pay zakat, fast Ramaḍān, and make pilgrimage to the House."

Then he said, "Shall I direct you to the gates of goodness? Fasting, which is a shield; charity, which extinguishes sin as water extinguishes fire; and prayer in the dead of the night." Then he recited, *Their sides shun their beds as they call upon their Lord in fear and hope, and they spend from what We have provided them. No soul knows what joy is kept in store for them as reward for what they used to do* [Q. 32:16–17].

Then he said, "Shall I tell you of the head, the pillar, and the pinnacle of the whole affair?" Muʿādh replied, "Please do, Messenger of God." He said, "The head is Islam, the pillar is prayer, and the pinnacle is struggle."

Then he said, "Shall I tell you the foundation of all that?" Muʿādh replied, "Please do, Messenger of God." He took hold of his tongue and said, "Restrain this."

Muʿādh said, "Prophet of God, shall we really be taken to account for our words?" He replied, "Woe betide you, Muʿādh! Will anything lead to people being dragged upon their faces (or he may have said "their noses") into Hell, more so than the things they say?" [Tirmidhī 2616]

Commentary

"Will anything lead to people being dragged upon their faces into Hell, more so than the things they say?" This refers to how people offend against one another by violating their honor with backbiting and tale-telling. The sins of the tongue are backbiting, tale-bearing, lying, slander, sacrilegious talk, jeering, and promise-breaking. God says, *It is most detestable in God's sight that you say what you do not do* [Q. 61:3].

HADITH 30

Keeping Within God's Boundaries

عَنْ أَبِي ثَعْلَبَةَ الْخُشَنِيِّ جُرْثُوْمِ بْنِ نَاشِر رَضِيَ اللّٰهُ عَنْهُ عَنْ رَسُوْلِ اللّٰهِ صَلَّى اللّٰهُ عَلَيْهِ وَسَلَّمَ قَالَ:

«إِنَّ اللّٰهَ تَعَالَى فَرَضَ فَرَائِضَ فَلَا تُضَيِّعُوْهَا، وَحَدَّ حُدُوْدًا فَلَا تَعْتَدُوْهَا، وَحَرَّمَ أَشْيَاءَ فَلَا تَنْتَهِكُوْهَا، وَسَكَتَ عَنْ أَشْيَاءَ رَحْمَةً لَكُمْ غَيْرَ نِسْيَانٍ فَلَا تَبْحَثُوا عَنْهَا».

Jurthum ibn Nāshir ﵁ related that the Messenger of God ﷺ said, "God has laid down obligations, so do not neglect them. He has set boundaries, so do not transgress them. He has forbidden things, so do not indulge in them. Then there are things He has not mentioned at all—out of mercy for you, not from forgetfulness—so do not go delving into them." [Dāraquṭnī 4814]

Commentary

Ibn Daqīq al-ʿĪd: Some scholars say that the Israelites used to ask every question they had and would always be answered, until this caused discord to arise among them, leading to their ruin. The Companions of the Prophet ﷺ understood this and refrained from asking questions unless it was necessary. They were always pleased to see Bedouins come to the Prophet ﷺ to ask questions, as this would be an opportunity for them to learn. Some have said that it is not permitted to ask scholars about theoretical matters at all. The early Muslims used to say of such questions, "Wait until it happens, then ask."

ASCETICISM

عَنْ أَبِي الْعَبَّاسِ سَهْلِ بْنِ سَعْدٍ السَّاعِدِيِّ رَضِيَ اللّٰهُ عَنْهُ قَالَ:
«جَاءَ رَجُلٌ إِلَى النَّبِيِّ صَلَّى اللّٰهُ عَلَيْهِ وَسَلَّمَ فَقَالَ: يَا رَسُولَ اللّٰهِ! دُلَّنِي
عَلَى عَمَلٍ إِذَا عَمِلْتُهُ أَحَبَّنِي اللّٰهُ وَأَحَبَّنِي النَّاسُ؛ فَقَالَ: «ازْهَدْ فِي الدُّنْيَا
يُحِبُّكَ اللّٰهُ، وَازْهَدْ فِيمَا عِنْدَ النَّاسِ يُحِبُّكَ النَّاسُ».

Sahl ibn Saʿd al-Sāʿidī ﷺ reported that,

"A man came to the Prophet ﷺ and said, Messenger of God, tell
me something I can do so that God will love me and people will
love me." He replied, "Be ascetic in this world, and God will love
you. Be undesirous of what other people have, and people will love
you." [Ibn Mājah 4102]

Commentary
Asceticism means to abstain from anything in the world that you do
not really need, even if it is lawful, and make do with what is sufficient.
It is said that the most intelligent people are the ascetics, for they love
everything that God loves and dislike everything that He dislikes, and
so they are at ease with themselves.

ʿUmar ﷺ said, "Dear God, we rejoice only in what You provide us." God praises those who live modestly when He says, *And [the servants of the All-Merciful are] those who, when they expend, are neither prodigal nor miserly but moderate between the two* [Q. 25:67]. The Prophet ﷺ said, "Those who seek God's guidance will not be disappointed; those who seek advice will not regret it; and those who are moderate will not be needy."

HADITH 32

Do No Harm

عَنْ أَبِيْ سَعِيْدٍ سَعْدِ بْنِ مَالِكِ بْنِ سِنَانٍ الْخُدْرِيِّ رَضِيَ اللّٰهُ عَنْهُ أَنَّ رَسُوْلَ اللّٰهِ صَلَّى اللّٰهُ عَلَيْهِ وَسَلَّمَ قَالَ:

«لَا ضَرَرَ وَلَا ضِرَارَ».

It is conveyed from Abū Saʿīd al-Khudrī ﷺ that the Messenger of God said ﷺ,

"Do no harm, and return no harm." [Ibn Mājah 2341, Dāraquṭnī 4539]

Commentary

Do not harm others unjustly or return harm that is done to you. If you are insulted, do not return the insult. If you are insulted, do not return the insult. If someone hits you, do not him but seek redress from the authorities. When two men trade insults or slander, this does not amount to lawful retribution. Rather, each of them should claim his right from the authorities. The Prophet ﷺ said, "When two people trade insults, they are responsible for what they say. The one who starts it bears the sin, as long as the injured party does not come up with a worse insult."

HADITH 33

The Burden of Proof

عَنِ ابْنِ عَبَّاسٍ رَضِيَ اللّٰهُ عَنْهُمَا أَنَّ رَسُوْلَ اللّٰهِ صَلَّى اللّٰهُ عَلَيْهِ وَسَلَّمَ قَالَ:
«لَوْ يُعْطَى النَّاسُ بِدَعْوَاهُمْ لَادَّعَى رِجَالٌ أَمْوَالَ قَوْمٍ وَدِمَاءَهُمْ، لَكِنَّ
الْبَيِّنَةَ عَلَى الْمُدَّعِي، وَالْيَمِينَ عَلَى مَنْ أَنْكَرَ».

Ibn ʿAbbās related that God's Messenger said,

"If people were given whatever they laid claim to, men would lay claim to the property and blood of others. But the burden of proof fails on the claimant, and one who denies the claim must swear an oath." [Bayhaqī, *Ṣughrā* 3386; shorter versions cited in Bukhārī 4552, Muslim 1711]

Commentary

The reason why the burden of proof is on the claimant is that he is the one making a claim that is contrary to outward appearances. There should always be presumption of innocence. The exception to this is when a person makes a claim about a private matter that only they could know, such as when a boy reaches puberty or a woman reaches the end of her waiting-period.

HADITH 34

Righting What is Wrong

عَنْ أَبِي سَعِيْدٍ الْخُدْرِيِّ رَضِيَ اللّٰهُ عَنْهُ قَالَ سَمِعْتُ رَسُوْلَ اللّٰهِ صَلَّى اللّٰهُ عَلَيْهِ وَسَلَّمَ يَقُوْلُ:

«مَنْ رَأَى مِنْكُمْ مُنْكَرًا فَلْيُغَيِّرْهُ بِيَدِهِ، فَإِنْ لَمْ يَسْتَطِعْ فَبِلِسَانِهِ، فَإِنْ لَمْ يَسْتَطِعْ فَبِقَلْبِهِ، وَذَلِكَ أَضْعَفُ الْإِيْمَانِ».

Abū Saʿīd al-Khudrī ﵁ related that he heard God's Messenger ﷺ say,

"Should any of you witness something that is wrong he should change it with his hand, or if he cannot then with his voice, or if he cannot then with his heart; and that is the weakest faith." [Muslim 49]

Commentary

This does not mean that when a powerless person condemns evil in his heart, his faith is weaker than that of others. What it means is that this is the lowest level of faith, for action is the fruit of faith. When it comes to enjoining what is right and forbidding what is wrong, the highest level of faith is to prevent the evil with one's own hand. If this should lead to death, then it is a martyr's death. Luqmān says in the

Qur'an, *O my son, observe prayer, and enjoin right and forbid wrong, and be patient through whatever may befall you* [Q. 31:17]. Someone who is able to condemn evil with his voice must do so even if he will not be heard. Likewise, even if you know that someone will not return your greeting of peace, you must still extend the greeting to them.

What does it mean to "change" evil with the heart? Surely one cannot change something by condemning it inwardly? What it means is to condemn the evil and disapprove of it, and to engage in the remembrance of God. God praises those who do so when He says, *When they come across vain talk, they pass by with dignity* [Q. 25:72].

HADITH 35

The Rights of One's Fellow Muslims

عَنْ أَبِيْ هُرَيْرَةَ رَضِيَ اللّٰهُ عَنْهُ قَالَ: قَالَ رَسُوْلُ اللّٰهِ صَلَّى اللّٰهُ عَلَيْهِ وَسَلَّمَ: «لَا تَحَاسَدُوْا، وَلَا تَنَاجَشُوْا، وَلَا تَبَاغَضُوْا، وَلَا تَدَابَرُوْا، وَلَا يَبِعْ بَعْضُكُمْ عَلَى بَيْعِ بَعْضٍ، وَكُونُوْا عِبَادَ اللّٰهِ إِخْوَانًا، الْمُسْلِمُ أَخُو الْمُسْلِمِ، لَا يَظْلِمُهُ، وَلَا يَخْذُلُهُ، وَلَا يَكْذِبُهُ، وَلَا يَحْقِرُهُ، التَّقْوَى هَاهُنَا، وَيُشِيْرُ إِلَى صَدْرِهِ ثَلَاثَ مَرَّاتٍ، بِحَسْبِ امْرِئٍ مِنَ الشَّرِّ أَنْ يَحْقِرَ أَخَاهُ الْمُسْلِمَ، كُلُّ الْمُسْلِمِ عَلَى الْمُسْلِمِ حَرَامٌ: دَمُهُ وَمَالُهُ وَعِرْضُهُ».

Abū Hurayra ﵁ reported that the Messenger of God ﷺ said,

"Do not envy one another; do not drive up prices for one another; do not hate one another; do not alienate one another; do not undercut one another. Be servants of God, brothers. A Muslim is his fellow Muslim's brother. He does not wrong him, betray him, or despise him. God-consciousness is here"—and he pointed to his chest three times. "It is evil enough for a man to look down on his

Muslim brother. The whole of every Muslim is inviolable to every other Muslim: his blood, his property, and his honor." [Muslim 2564]

Commentary

The Prophet ﷺ said, "It is not permitted fora Muslim to shun his brother for more than three days, each of them turning away whenever they meet. The better man is the one who greets the other first."

"A Muslim is his fellow Muslim's brother. He does not wrong him, betray him, or despise him." He does not judge himself better than his fellow, but holds himself to be worse—or he does not judge at all, for none of us know how things will turn out in the end. When you see a younger person, remember that he has fewer sins than you. When you see an older person, remember that he is your senior in Islam. When you see a non-Muslim, do not be certain that he is bound for Hell, for he may embrace Islam and die a Muslim.

He ﷺ proclaimed that every Muslim's blood, property, and honor are sacrosanct during his sermon at the Farewell Pilgrimage.

HADITH 36

Helping Others and Seeking Knowledge

عَنْ أَبِي هُرَيْرَةَ رَضِيَ اللّٰهُ عَنْهُ عَنِ النَّبِيِّ صَلَّى اللّٰهُ عَلَيْهِ وَسَلَّمَ قَالَ:

«مَنْ نَفَّسَ عَنْ مُؤْمِنٍ كُرْبَةً مِنْ كُرَبِ الدُّنْيَا نَفَّسَ اللّٰهُ عَنْهُ كُرْبَةً مِنْ كُرَبِ يَوْمِ الْقِيَامَةِ، وَمَنْ يَسَّرَ عَلَى مُعْسِرٍ، يَسَّرَ اللّٰهُ عَلَيْهِ فِي الدُّنْيَا وَالْآخِرَةِ، وَمَنْ سَتَرَ مُسْلِمًا سَتَرَهُ اللّٰهُ فِي الدُّنْيَا وَالْآخِرَةِ ، وَاللّٰهُ فِي عَوْنِ الْعَبْدِ مَا كَانَ الْعَبْدُ فِي عَوْنِ أَخِيْهِ، وَمَنْ سَلَكَ طَرِيْقًا يَلْتَمِسُ فِيْهِ عِلْمًا سَهَّلَ اللّٰهُ لَهُ بِهِ طَرِيْقًا إِلَى الْجَنَّةِ، وَمَا اجْتَمَعَ قَوْمٌ فِي بَيْتٍ مِنْ بُيُوْتِ اللّٰهِ يَتْلُوْنَ كِتَابَ اللّٰهِ، وَيَتَدَارَسُوْنَهُ فِيْمَا بَيْنَهُمْ؛ إِلَّا نَزَلَتْ عَلَيْهِمُ السَّكِيْنَةُ، وَغَشِيَتْهُمُ الرَّحْمَةُ، وَحَفَّتْهُمُ المَلَائِكَةُ، وَذَكَرَهُمُ اللّٰهُ فِيْمَنْ عِنْدَهُ، وَمَنْ أَبْطَأَ بِهِ عَمَلُهُ لَمْ يُسْرِعْ بِهِ نَسَبُهُ».

Abū Hurayra ﷺ related that the Prophet ﷺ said,

"Whoever eases the suffering of a believer in this world, God will ease his suffering on the Day of Resurrection. Whoever helps a person in difficulty, God will grant him ease in this life and the Next. Whoever conceals a Muslim's blemish, God will conceal his in this life and the Next. God helps His servant as long as the servant helps his brother. Whoever follows a path in pursuit of knowledge, God will lead him gently along a path to Paradise. Whenever a group of people gather in one of God's houses to recite God's Book and study it among themselves, tranquility descends upon them, mercy envelops them, and angels surround them. God mentions them to those who are with Him. Whoever's deeds slow him down, his lineage will not speed him up." [Muslim 2699]

Commentary

This hadith shows that it is recommended to give loans, and to rescue a Muslim from captivity by paying their ransom or bail. It is said that when Joseph ﷺ was released from prison, he wrote upon the door, "This is the grave of the living, the curse of the enemy, and the trial of the righteous."

Another lesson of the hadith is that if you witness a sin you should keep it secret. God says, *Truly those who love to see slander spread against those who believe shall have a painful punishment in the present life and the Hereafter* [Q. 24:19]. Some say that even those who witness adultery should keep it secret rather than testifying, or that they should only testify if there is a good reason to do so.

The hadith also shows the merit of travelling in pursuit of knowledge. It is related that God told David ﷺ to take up a staff of iron and don shoes of iron, and to walk in pursuit of knowledge until they were worn out. Of course, it is essential to act upon the knowledge that you acquire, and to teach it to others. You must not take pride in your knowledge, nor be stingy with it. Nor must you be afraid to admit when you do not know something. You must be humble, and be prepared to bear what hardship may come your way as a result of the advice you give to others. You must teach those who are most in need of learning first, just as you give charity to the most needy recipients.

"When a group of people gather in one of God's houses to recite God's Book and study it among themselves, tranquility descends upon them, mercy envelops them, and angels surround them. God mentions them to those who are with Him." God says, *Truly it is in the remembrance of God that hearts find peace* [Q. 13:28]. It is enough to show the honor of remembrance of God that one who engages in it is mentioned by God among the Supreme Assembly.

"If a person's deeds slow him down, his lineage will not speed him up." It is righteous actions that count, not noble lineage, God says, *Truly the noblest of you in God's sight are the most God-fearing of you* [Q. 49:13].

HADITH 37

God's Kindness

عَنِ ابْنِ عَبَّاسٍ رَضِيَ اللّٰهُ عَنْهُمَا عَنْ رَسُوْلِ اللّٰهِ صَلَّى اللّٰهُ عَلَيْهِ وَسَلَّمَ فِيْمَا يَرْوِيْهِ عَنْ رَبِّهِ تَبَارَكَ وَتَعَالَى، قَالَ:

«إِنَّ اللّٰهَ كَتَبَ الْحَسَنَاتِ وَالسَّيِّئَاتِ، ثُمَّ بَيَّنَ ذَلِكَ، فَمَنْ هَمَّ بِحَسَنَةٍ فَلَمْ يَعْمَلْهَا كَتَبَهَا اللّٰهُ عِنْدَهُ حَسَنَةً كَامِلَةً، وَإِنْ هَمَّ بِهَا فَعَمِلَهَا كَتَبَهَا اللّٰهُ عِنْدَهُ عَشْرَ حَسَنَاتٍ إِلَى سَبْعِمِائَةِ ضِعْفٍ إِلَى أَضْعَافٍ كَثِيْرَةٍ، وَإِنْ هَمَّ بِسَيِّئَةٍ فَلَمْ يَعْمَلْهَا كَتَبَهَا اللّٰهُ عِنْدَهُ حَسَنَةً كَامِلَةً، وَإِنْ هَمَّ بِهَا فَعَمِلَهَا كَتَبَهَا اللّٰهُ سَيِّئَةً وَاحِدَةً».

Ibn ʿAbbās ﵄ related from the Prophet ﷺ that he conveyed the following from his Lord, Blessed and Exalted is He:

"God has written down all good and evil deeds, and has made this plain. If someone is intent upon a good deed but does not do it, God records it in His Presence as one full good deed. If he is intent upon it and does it, God records it in His Presence as from ten good deeds up to seven hundred times, or even more. If he is intent upon an evil deed but does not do it, God records it in His Presence as one full good deed. If he is intent upon it and does it, God recordsit as a single evil deed." [Bukhārī 6491, Muslim 131]

Commentary

Behold God's tremendous kindness! He writes the deed down "in His Presence", such is the attention He affords it, and writes it "full" to emphasize it. Yet the single evil deed that He records is not emphasized in that way. Praise be to God! We cannot praise and glorify Him enough. All thanks is due to Him, and all blessings and grace are from Him.

HADITH 38

The Friends of God

عَنْ أَبِي هُرَيْرَةَ رَضِيَ اللّٰهُ عَنْهُ قَالَ: قَالَ رَسُوْلُ اللّٰهِ صَلَّى اللّٰهُ عَلَيْهِ وَسَلَّمَ
إِنَّ اللّٰهَ تَعَالَى قَالَ:

«مَنْ عَادَى لِيْ وَلِيًّا فَقَدْ آذَنْتُهُ بِالْحَرْبِ، وَمَا تَقَرَّبَ إِلَيَّ عَبْدِي بِشَيْءٍ أَحَبَّ إِلَيَّ مِمَّا افْتَرَضْتُهُ عَلَيْهِ، وَلَا يَزَالُ عَبْدِي يَتَقَرَّبُ إِلَيَّ بِالنَّوَافِلِ حَتَّى أُحِبَّهُ، فَإِذَا أَحْبَبْتُهُ كُنْتُ سَمْعَهُ الَّذِي يَسْمَعُ بِهِ، وَبَصَرَهُ الَّذِي يُبْصِرُ بِهِ، وَيَدَهُ الَّتِي يَبْطِشُ بِهَا، وَرِجْلَهُ الَّتِي يَمْشِي بِهَا، وَلَئِنْ سَأَلَنِي لَأُعْطِيَنَّهُ، وَلَئِنْ اسْتَعَاذَنِي لَأُعِيذَنَّهُ».

Abū Hurayra ؓ reported that the Messenger of God ﷺ related that God Almighty says:

"If anyone attacks a friend of Mine, I declare war upon him. My servant cannot draw nearer to Me with anything I love more than the duties I have assigned him; and My servant continues to draw near to me with voluntary deeds until I love him. When I love him, I become his hearing with which he hears, his sight with which he sees, his hand with which he grasps, and his foot with which he walks. Were he to ask of Me, I would certainly give to him; and were he to seek refuge with Me, I would certainly grant him refuge." [Bukhārī 6502]

Commentary

The friend of God here means the believer. As God says, *God is the Friend of those who believe* [Q. 2:257]. God declares war upon anyone who attacks a believer; and when God wages war on someone He destroys them utterly. Thus you must take great pains to avoid harming any Muslim.

"My servant cannot draw nearer to Me with anything I love more than the duties I have assigned him." This proves that obligatory deeds are superior to voluntary ones; according to another hadith they are seventy times better.

"My servant continues to draw near to me with voluntary deeds until I love him." God's love is His desire for good; when He loves His servant, He busies him with remembrance of Him and obedience to Him and protects him from Satan, and He engages his body in obedience to Him. He causes him to prefer the sound of the Qur'an, and invocation to the sound of profane music. He protects his sight from forbidden things and directs it towards contemplation and reflection, so that everything he sees reminds him of its Creator. ʿAlī ﷺ said, "I see nothing without seeing God before it." Through this vision, contemplation of created things lead to realization of the omnipotent power of the Creator. All the movements of his hands and feet become sacred and devoted to God, and are rewarded accordingly. Nothing he does is in vain; all is for God.

HADITH 39

God's Clemency

عَنِ ابْنِ عَبَّاسٍ رَضِيَ اللّٰهُ عَنْهُمَا أَنَّ رَسُوْلَ اللّٰهِ صَلَّى اللّٰهُ عَلَيْهِ وَسَلَّمَ قَالَ:

«إِنَّ اللّٰهَ تَجَاوَزَ لِيْ عَنْ أُمَّتِي الْخَطَأَ وَالنِّسْيَانَ وَمَا اسْتُكْرِهُوا عَلَيْهِ».

Ibn ʿAbbās ﷺ reported that the Messenger of God ﷺ said,

"God has undertaken for my sake to pardon my Community for their mistakes, their forgetfulness, and anything that they are forced to do." [Ibn Mājah 2045, Bayhaqī 15094]

Commentary

This applies to the sin itself, but not to the legal ruling where other parties are involved. If you are given something to look after and then you accidentally lose it, you must still compensate the owner for it. Nor does adultery or murder become lawful if one is compelled to commit it. Forgetfulness might also be inexcusable if a person has not taken the proper precautions to remind himself. One could write an entire book about the implications of this one hadith.

HADITH 40

Living in the Moment

عَنِ ابْنِ عُمَرَ رَضِيَ اللّٰهُ عَنْهُمَا قَالَ: أَخذَ رَسُوْلُ اللّٰهِ صَلَّى اللّٰهُ عَلَيْهِ وَسَلَّمَ بِمَنْكِبِي، وَقَالَ:

«كُنْ فِي الدُّنْيَا كَأَنَّك غَرِيْبٌ أَوْ عَابِرُ سَبِيْلٍ».

وَكَانَ ابْنُ عُمَرَ رَضِيَ اللّٰهُ عَنْهُمَا يَقُوْلُ:

«إِذَا أَمْسَيْتَ فَلَا تَنْتَظِرِ الصَّبَاحَ، وَإِذَا أَصْبَحْتَ فَلَا تَنْتَظِرِ الْمَسَاءَ، وَخُذْ مِنْ صِحَّتِكَ لِمَرَضِكَ، وَمِنْ حَيَاتِكَ لِمَوْتِكَ».

Ibn ʿUmar ﷺ reported that the Messenger of God ﷺ grasped him by the shoulder and said,

"Be in this world like a stranger or a passer-by."

Ibn ʿUmar ﷺ used to say,

"When evening comes ,do not expect to see the morning; and when morning comes, do not expect to see the evening. Make the most of your health before you fall sick, and make the most of your life before you die." [Bukhārī 6416]

Commentary

"Be in this world like a stranger or a traveler." Do not become at home in it, nor suggest to yourself that you might remain in it, nor become attached to it any more than a stranger becomes attached to a foreign land when he yearns to return to his home and family. Salmān al-Fārisī ⁕ said, "My dear friend ⁕ told me not to take anything from the world except as a traveler takes provisions."

A poet said, "Do you hope to remain in a place that cannot endure? Have you ever heard of a shadow that did not move?"

The hadith shows that we should not look too far to the future, but repent and prepare for death. If you do look to the future, always say "God willing." God says, *And never say of anything 'I will do this tomorrow' without adding 'If God will'* [Q. 18:23–24].

Al-Ghazālī said that a man's body is like a net in which he catches righteous deeds. When he dies, he will no longer need the net. Upon death a person will lose all desire for the world and desire only righteous deeds, for they will be the provision he takes to the grave. If he does not have any, he will ask to be sent back to the world to collect some. *And when death comes to one of them, he says, 'My Lord, send me back, that I may work righteousness in what I left behind'* [Q. 23:99–100]. But then it will be too late, for his net will have been taken from him, and he will have nothing but regrets. Therefore the Prophet ⁕ said, "Make the most of your life before you die." And there is no power or strength except through God, the Exalted, the Immense.

HADITH 41

FOLLOWING THE PROPHET ﷺ

عَنْ أَبِي مُحَمَّدٍ عَبْدِ اللّٰهِ بْنِ عَمْرِو بْنِ الْعَاصِ رَضِيَ اللّٰهُ عَنْهُمَا، قَالَ: قَالَ
رَسُوْلُ اللّٰهِ صَلَّى اللّٰهُ عَلَيْهِ وَسَلَّمَ:

«لَا يُؤْمِنُ أَحَدُكُمْ حَتَّى يَكُوْنَ هَوَاهُ تَبَعًا لِمَا جِئْتُ بِهِ».

ʿAmr ibn al-ʿĀṣ ﷺ reported that the Messenger of God ﷺ said,

"None of you is a true believer until his desires conform to what I have brought." [Ibn Abī ʿĀṣim, 15]

Commentary

You must refer your actions to the Qur'an and Sunna, and oppose our vain desires. God says, *It is not for any believing man or woman, when God and His Messenger have decreed a matter, to have any choice in the matter* [Q. 33:36].

HADITH 42

The Vastness of God's Mercy

عَنْ أَنَسِ بْنِ مَالِكٍ رَضِيَ اللّٰهُ عَنْهُ قَالَ: سَمِعْتُ رَسُوْلَ اللّٰهِ صَلَّى اللّٰهُ عَلَيْهِ
وَسَلَّمَ يَقُوْلُ: قَالَ اللّٰهُ تَعَالَى:

«يَا ابْنَ آدَمَ! إِنَّكَ مَا دَعَوْتَنِي وَرَجَوْتَنِي غَفَرْتُ لَكَ عَلَى مَا كَانَ مِنْكَ
وَلَا أُبَالِيْ، يَا ابْنَ آدَمَ! لَوْ بَلَغَتْ ذُنُوْبُكَ عَنَانَ السَّمَاءِ ثُمَّ اسْتَغْفَرْتَنِيْ غَفَرْتُ
لَكَ، يَا ابْنَ آدَمَ! إِنَّكَ لَوْ أَتَيْتَنِيْ بِقُرَابِ الْأَرْضِ خَطَايَا ثُمَّ لَقِيْتَنِيْ لَا تُشْرِكُ
بِيْ شَيْئًا لَأَتَيْتُكَ بِقُرَابِهَا مَغْفِرَةً».

Anas ibn Mālik رضي الله عنه reported that he heard the Messenger of God ﷺ state that God Almighty says,

"Child of Adam, as long as You call upon Me and place your hope in Me, I will forgive you for whatever you do, and I will not care! Child of Adam, if your sins piled up to the clouds and then you asked forgiveness of Me, I would forgive you. Child of Adam, if you came to Me with sins enough to fill the earth but met Me without associating any partners with Me, I would grant you forgiveness enough to fill the earth." [Tirmidhī 3540]

Commentary

God says, *Whoever does evil or wrongs himself, and then asks forgiveness of God, shall find God Forgiving, Merciful* [Q. 4:110]. The first level of asking forgiveness is to ask God to forgive one's sins, which is the petition of the sinful. The second level is to ask Him to forgive one's shortcomings in being thankful to Him, which is the petition of the righteous. The third level is a pure expression of thanks, which was the petition of the Messenger of God ﷺ and all the other Prophets, may peace and blessings be upon them all.

The Prophet ﷺ said that the foremost of all prayers for forgiveness is, "Dear God, You are my Lord; there is no god but You. You created me, and I am Your servant, and I hold to Your covenant and Your promise as far as I am able. I seek refuge with You from the evil I have done. I acknowledge to You Your favor, and I confess my sin. Forgive me, for none can forgive sins but You."

He ﷺ also taught Abū Bakr ؓ to say, "Dear God, I have wronged myself much (or, in another narration, "greatly"), and none can forgive sins but You. Grant me forgiveness from Yourself, and have mercy upon me. Truly You are the Forgiving, the Merciful."

This brings to an end that which God, the Noble and Generous, has enabled me to compile in a concise form. Praise be to God, the Lord of the Worlds.

Hadith Sources

Bayhaqī, Aḥmad ibn Ḥusayn, *al-Sunan al-Ṣaghīr*, Islamic University of Karachi, 1989

Bukhārī, Muḥammad ibn Ismāʿīl, *Ṣaḥīḥ*, Dar Ṭawq al-Najāh, 1422 AH

Dāraquṭnī, ʿAlī ibn ʿUmar, *Sunan*, Muʾassasa al-Risāla, Beirut 2004

Nasāʾī, Aḥmad ibn Shuʿayb, *Sunan*, Maktab al-Maṭbūʿāt al-Islāmiyya, Aleppo 1986

Nīsābūrī, Muslim ibn Ḥajjāj, *Ṣaḥīḥ*, Dār Iḥyāʾ al-Turāth al-ʿArabī, Beirut

Qazwīnī, Ibn Mājah, *Sunan*, Dār Iḥyāʾ al-Kutub al-ʿArabiyya

Shaybānī, Ibn Abī ʿĀṣim, *al-Sunna*, al-Maktab al-Islāmī, Beirut 1400 AH

Sijistānī, Abū Dāwūd Sulaymān, *Sunan*, al-Maktaba al-ʿAṣriyya, Beirut

Tirmidhī, Muḥammad ibn ʿĪsā, *Sunan*, Dār al-Gharb al-Islāmī, Beirut 1998

Endnotes

ABOUT THE AUTHOR

1. Muḥammad b. Aḥmad b. ʿUthmān al-Dhahabī, *Tārīkh al-Islām wa wafayāt al-mashāhīr wa'l-aʿlām* (Beirut: Dār al-Kitāb al-ʿArabī, 2003), 50:246.
2. Muḥammad b. Aḥmad b. ʿUthmān al-Dhahabī, *Tadhkirat al-ḥuffāẓ* (Beirut: Dār al-Kutub al-ʿIlmiyya, 1998), 4:1473.
3. ʿAlāʾ al-Dīn Ibn al-ʿAṭṭār, *Tarjamat al-Imām Muḥyī al-Dīn al-Nawawī* (Riyadh: Dār al-Samiʿa, 1993), 1.
4. Al-Subkī, Tāj al-Dīn ʿAbd al-Wahhāb *Ṭabaqāt al-Shāfiʿiyya al-kubrā* (Beirut: Dār al-Kutub al-ʿIlmiyya, 1999), 4:471.
5. Ismāʿīl b. ʿUmar Ibn Kathīr, *al-Bidāyawa al-nihāya* (Beirut: Dār Iḥyāʾ al-Turāth al-ʿArabī, 2001), 13:278.
6. al-Diqr, *al-Imām al-Nawawī*, 27.
7. Ibid., 35.
8. al-Subkī, *Ṭabaqāt al-Shāfiʿiyya*, 4:306.
9. That is, the Levant, comprising modern Syria, Israel, Jordan, Lebanon, and the Palestinian territories.
10. al-Diqr, *al-Imām al-Nawawī*, 37–46.
11. Amjad Rashīd, *Imām Nawawī's Role in the Shāfiʿī School* (http://qa.sunnipath. com).
12. ʿAbd al-Raḥīm al-Asnawī, *al-Ṭabaqāt al-Shāfiʿiyya* (Beirut: Dār al-Kutub al-ʿIlmiyya, 1987), 2:66.
13. al-Diqr, *al-Imām al-Nawawī*, 50.
14. Ibid., 59.
15. Ibn al-ʿAṭṭār, *Tarjama*, 8.
16. al-Dhahabī, *Tadhkirat al-ḥuffāẓ*, 4:1472.
17. Muslim b. al-Ḥajjāj al-Qushayrī, *Jāmiʿ al-ṣaḥīḥ: Sharḥ Muslim*

bi-sharḥ al-Nawawī, ed. ʿIṣām al-Dīn al-Ṣabābiṭī (Cairo: Dār al-Ḥadīth, 1994).

18. Ibn al-ʿAṭṭār, *Tarjama*, 9.
19. al-Nawawī, *al-Taqrīb fī uṣūl al-ḥadīth* (Beirut: Dār al-Turāth al-ʿArabī, 1981), 25.
20. Ibn al-ʿAṭṭār, *Tarjama*, 12.
21. al-Diqr, *al-Imām al-Nawawī*, 70.
22. Ibid., 66.
23. Ibid., 65.
24. For a list of both completed and incomplete books written by Imām al-Nawawī, see Rafik Berjak, *Al-Nawawī, the Jurist of Islam* (Victoria, BC: Trafford, 2007), 115–135.
25. Ibn al-ʿAṭṭār, *Tarjama*, 90.
26. Ibn Kathīr, *al-Bidāya*, 13:279.
27. al-Diqr, *al-Imām al-Nawawī*, 89.
28. Ibid., 103.
29. Cf. Nuh Keller, *al-Maqasid: Imam Nawawi's Manual of Islam* (Evanston, IN: Sunna Books, 1994), 85–86, with slight amendments to the translation.
30. al-Nawawī, *Sharḥ Ṣaḥīḥ Muslim*, 10:77.
31. al-Diqr, *al-Imām al-Nawawī*, 108.
32. Ibid.
33. Ibid., 142–43. These verses are quoted from Ibn al-ʿAṭṭār and al-Diqr and translated by Rafik Berjak.

CPSIA information can be obtained
at www.ICGtesting.com
Printed in the USA
BVHW051842070822
643859BV00001B/8

9 781939 256096